SEVENTH SENSE

SEVENTH SENSE

Sunny Thomas

ISPCK/CNI/LMCC
2006

Seventh Sense – Published by the Rev. Ashish Amos of the Indian Society for Promoting Christian Knowledge (ISPCK), Post Box 1585, Kashmere Gate, Delhi-110006 for Church of North India (CNI), Literature & Mass Communication Committee (LMCC).

© Author, 2006

All rights reserved. No part of this book may be reproduced or transmitted in any form or by any means, electronic, mechanical, photocopying, recording, or by any information storage and retrieval system, without the prior permission in writing from the publisher.

The views expressed in the Book are that of the author and the publisher takes no responsibility of any of the statements.

ISBN: 81-7214-918-2

Cover idea : **NEELAB**

Book design : VIRENDRA SINGH

Laser typeset by **ISPCK,** Post Box 1585, 1654 Madarsa Road, Kashmere Gate, Delhi-110006
Tel: 23866323, *Fax:* 91-11-23865490.
e-mail: ashish@ispck.org.in • mail@ispck.org.in
website: www.ispck.org.in

Dedicated

To

Anna Mol

CONTENTS

Dedication v
Acknowledgements xi
One Solitary Life xiii
Read Me xv
Decoding the Da Vinci Code Lies xix

Book One

The Website Of God 1
The Wrath Of Herod 7
Behold The Lamb Of God 20
The Wine Of Cana 29

Book Two

The New Life 33
The Living Water 37
Capernaum The New Home 41
The Lake Of Galilee 44
    In Jerusalem 47
Holiness Of The Foxes 50

Book Three

The Architects Of The Kingdom 52
The Sermon On The Mount 57
Faith Heals 68

The Pharisee's Dinner. 71
Deceiver Or Messiah? 75
The Good Samaritan 80

Book Four

The Bread Of Life 84
O Woman, Great Is Your Faith 90
'Who Do You Say I Am?' 94
Transfiguration 97
The Kingdom Within You 99
The Blind See 103
The Good Shepherd 106
Deadman Lazarus 111
Take Up Your Cross 115
Father's Love 119
Zacchaeus Sees Jesus 122

Book Five

Triumphal Entry 125
The Second Cleansing 130
    Monday 130
    Tuesday 131
By Whose Authority? 132
Battle Of Wits 137
Woe To You Pharisees! 142
Sermon On Resurrection 146
The Second Coming 148
The Last Parables 151

Book Six

The Passover Lamb	155
The Troubled Hearts	166
The True Vine	173
The World Hates You	177
The Counsellor God	180
The High Priestly Prayer	182
The Longest Night	186
Judgement	193

Book Seven

The King Of The Jews	198
Conversion On The Cross	204
Behold Your Mother	207
My God, My God…!	209
It Is Finished	212
Blood And Water	214
Seeing Is Believing	217
The Unique Presence	227
The Roadmap To The Kingdom	229

Acknowledgements

I can easily compile a Who's Who of people whom I am indebted to while preparing this book. But a few names deserve to be mentioned, the first among them: Mr R. Sundar and Mr Arun Bahl, Directors of Bennett, Coleman & Co. Principal, Times School of Journalism (TSJ) Vispy R Saher has offered valuable comments after glancing through parts of the manuscript; Vice-Principal (TSJ) Rajesh K. Rattan has always been a pillar of strength.

I am indebted to Ashish Amos for encouraging me right from the beginning; and to Ella Sonawane for the value addition and revision of the manuscript, without which the book would not have been what it is.

I am grateful to my Walking Dictionary (wife) and to my daughter Sherry who comes up with ideas or suggests changes in my writing. My son Roy and daughter-in-law Rose have been constantly encouraging me from Houston, Texas (USA).

My understanding was broadened after I read Alfred Edersheim's book on Jesus Christ; and Secrets of the Code, edited by Dan Burstein (Published by Orion House, London); and The Truth Behind the Da Vinci Code By Richard Abanes (Published by Harvest House Publishers, Eugene, Oregon (USA), all of which I have quoted.

One Solitary Life

He was born in an obscure village, the child of
a peasant woman.

He grew up in still another village, where he worked
in a carpenter's shop until he was thirty...

Then for three years he was an itinerant preacher.
He never wrote a book. He never held any office. He
never had a family or owned a house.
He didn't go to a college.

He never visited a big city. He never travelled two
hundred miles from the place where he was born.
He did none of the things one usually
associate with greatness.

He had no credentials but himself. He was only
thirty-three when the tide of public opinion turned

against him. His friends ran away. He was turned
to his enemies and went through the mockery of
a trial. He was nailed to a cross between two thieves.

While he was dying, his executioners gambled for
his clothing, the only property he had on earth. When
he was dead, he was laid in a borrowed grave
through the pity of a friend.

Nineteen centuries have come and gone,
and today he is the central figure of
the human race and the leader of mankind's progress.

All the armies that ever marched, all the navies that
ever sailed, all the parliamentarians that ever sat, all the
kings that ever reigned put together, have not
affected the life of man on this earth as much as
that one solitary life.

READ ME

Every century is unique in its own way. The 21st century is amazing for its speed of communication and knowledge at the click of a mouse. Yet the 21st century is frightening for its lawless brigand striking in any part of the world targeting women and innocent children. The 21st century is disturbing for success has replaced truth, image and character. The shine and the sheen outside matters to us more than the inside which may be rotten. We dote on smart guys and smart girls, no matter whether they are the Uriah Heep awaiting the apocalyptical hour (time servers). Deception has become a major industry commanding respect — in politics, media, industry and on the market — and the gullible are drawn like rats to the music of the pied-piper.

What has religion got to do with the 21st century — except as a weapon of mass destruction? Religion is more powerful than the atom bomb that devastated Hiroshima and Nagasaki. The only difference is while the atom bomb destroys the enemy religion destroys one's own people. Religion for the quest for truth is replaced by religion for hatred. The comfort of religion is this that it answers questions that baffle all of us. It offers festivals for gaiety lovers, observances for slaves of habit, freedom for emancipation seeks, and philosophies for people who love to contemplate. Only the down right fool, intellectual or hedonist, can be an atheist.

"Did he really live," asked Napoleon — the first question he asked — on reaching Palestine. The life of Christ has fascinated humanity for the right and wrong reasons. So much has been written by so many over so much of time that one could almost be confused. Sensuous writers see him as a man of flesh and blood, lunatic philosophers consider him as one of their kindred, power-hungry politicians think he was one of them subtly trying to liberate his people. Some even consider him as a mythical character notwithstanding the historicity of records he has left behind. The debate whether Jesus Christ was a Catholic or a Protestant could split Christendom.

Malcolm Muggeridge was an atheist and a Marxist when he visited the Church of Nativity, which is the birthplace of Jesus Christ in Bethlehem. BBC has commissioned him to do a documentary and suddenly he could feel the place is different from any other place he had visited so far as a world-famous journalist. He could see before him all the events starting from the birth to the death and ascension of Jesus, as if seeing on a television screen. From an atheist he became an ardent believer who authored two books on Christ after considerable research.

Young boy Sunder decided to end his life by jumping in front of an express train that passed by his village hours before the dawn. Sunder prayed the whole night and the appointed time for his suicide was drawing near. As minutes dragged by, he saw a bright light in his room. Sunder knelt down and prayed, and asked, 'Who are you, Lord'. The answer came, 'I am Jesus of Nazareth'. He is the famous Sadhu Sunder Singh.

No matter what faith you belong to, reading this book will broaden your spiritual perspective. Many management gurus today write bestsellers adapting principles from the Sermon on the Mount and creating paradigms with spellbinding nomenclatures. Read with an open heart, the teaching of Christ will influence — whether you take it literally, intellectually or spiritually.

You must write a book like *Freedom at Midnight*, admonished a critic from my fraternity after he saw my small success in getting two books published. He suggested I should do a book on Jesus Christ. The idea somehow caught on my imagination and I started reading and collecting material for the book. The year was 1977 but the book never got started. After many false starts the book still remained a non-starter for a quarter of a decade.

'Don't unless you know the man,' warned the late John Dorsey, my friend and founder of Faith Academy School, New Delhi. I poured over almost all the books on Christ but the one that did course correction was by Michael Grant, a historian by profession. Like most historians and intellectuals, Grant was interested in finding something original, whether there is some grain of truth or not. Christ got himself betrayed by Judas because he could not accomplish his mission (now a promising bestseller has hit the market on this line); Christ never did any miracles; Christ was not born in Bethlehem; there came no wise men which is a figment of imagination; Christ deliberately did things to fulfil prophecies, thus goes the Grant book. The stretching out Grant has to do and the lack of cogent reasoning which is striking when you read the gospel accounts convinced me that Jesus was no ordinary man. Bertrand Russell's *Why Am I Not A Christian* further convinced my conviction that Russell has nothing more than his towering ego to offer. Some intellectuals suffer from the illusion that faith is intellectually inferior to atheism because worshipping something superior makes one inferior.

I miss (H. G.) Dr Paulose Mar Gregorios' critical comments, which would have strengthened this book. And finally, I am grateful to Dan Brown, without whom this book would have lost its relevance.

SUNNY THOMAS

New Delhi

DECODING THE DA VINCI CODE LIES

Behind every deception, there are truths, facts and fabrications. It is this cocktail that makes the deception deadlier for the gullible. In the name of research and scientific enquiry, all fabrications are done. There is a documentary released recently that claims man never landed on Moon, which ends with casting aspersions on John F Kennedy's assassination trial, emotionally linking a scientific enquiry with a political tragedy that caught on the imagination of our time.

Joseph Pulitzer is a legend of American Journalism. The Americans wanted a documentary made on him and they approached the Hungarian state television channel because he was a Hungarian émigré. When the documentary was finally made and shown to the Americans, they commented: "But there is no sex."

"That's the kind of life Pulitzer led," remonstrated the Director.

"That's all right for Hungarians. But we are Americans."

In came sex and out went truth. Some people believe sex is omnipresent. So Dan Brown, the author of *The Da Vinci Code*, introduced sex. He introduced not only sex but Isaac Newton, Victor Hugo, Botticelli and others to gain credibility for enterprise fabrication.

Brown believes that Leonardo da Vinci communicates to posterity through coded messages hidden in the three paintings

— 'Mona Lisa', the 'Last Supper' and the 'Virgin of Rocks' — which smart people like him were able to decode and — he could amass a royalty. The reason for the coded message is, of course, the fear of Inquisition of the church. Brown sees in Leonardo's 'Last Supper' Mary Magdalene sitting next to Jesus in place of St John the Beloved Disciple. Brown also sees a V-shape symbolic of Female Deity worship, next to Jesus.

Cloud-watching is the hobby of some people, who see at times a rabbit in the sky; others see Abraham Lincoln, Charlie Chaplin or Mahatma Gandhi; some others see Princess Diana, Marilyn Monroe or Jacqueline Kennedy. What you see in the cloud is a projection of your mind, and what Brown saw in the 'Last Supper' is a figment of his fertile imaginative mind.

The Last Supper is the most cherished and sacred moment in the life of the Apostles and that of the church, when Jesus Christ instituted the Holy Communion. It is well documented by eyewitnesses — by St John himself and by St Matthew, both of whom were Apostles of Christ chosen to bear witness. In fact, St. John records every moment in the Upper Room and every conversation. But there was no mention of Mary Magdalene in all his five chapters. Neither did St Matthew who had a sharp eye for details. Nor did John Mark who records Peter's memory — the very memory of the man designated to lead the flock after the Master's Ascension. Nor did Luke the Physician who investigated the truth of the origin of the gospel from all possible eyewitnesses.

When a fiction writer takes inspiration from a millionaire or a celebrity and weaves a story around him, the author will preface it by saying, "The characters in the book are fictitious and have no resemblance whatsoever with someone living or dead."

Similarly, when a fiction writer wants his readers to believe what he imagined or fabricated is true, he will write something like, "All descriptions of artwork, architecture, documents, and secret rituals in this novel are accurate". So does Brown at the beginning of his book. The average reader assumes the statement to be true. The fictitious characters, British historian Leigh Teabing

Decoding The Da Vinci Code Lies

and Harvard Professor Robert Langdon who teaches religious symbology, lend an aura of respectability. The reader assumes he is in learned company, forgetting they are creatures of imagination.

And most of what Brown tells us about Jesus, the Bible and early church history are simply not true. Through the mouth of the fictional historian, Brown suggests that "Constantine commissioned and financed a new Bible, which omitted those gospels that spoke of Christ's human traits and embellished those gospels that made him godlike."

Constantine had ordered fifty copies of the sacred scriptures from church historian Eusebius. To assume that the emperor decreed revision and embellishment of the gospels is pure fiction. A church that faced persecution for three centuries for faith in Jesus Christ would suddenly jettison the gospel and join in a grand conspiracy with Constantine is stretching one's imagination too far.

We have complete copies of both Luke and John dating between AD 175 and 225, and there is not a shred of evidence to suggest that embellishment of any kind has taken place. In fact, the strongest declarations of Jesus' deity are recoded in the earliest existing copies.

"Almost everything our fathers taught us about Christ is false!" That's true Dan Brown speaking through his fictitious historian Teabing. We will see how slippery is the ground on which Brown stands. But first the Brown story.

* * *

True Christianity was started by a prophet who made no claims to divinity. Married Mary Magdalene, he chose his wife to lead the church after him, but Peter usurped her authority and she was forced to flee Jerusalem. Virtually everyone knew this in the first century. In France, Mary gave birth to Jesus' daughter. The two outcasts remained in hiding for the rest of their lives. Meanwhile Peter turned a goddess-worshipping church into a Jesus-worshipping den of evildoers. Peter had a political agenda, too.

The true story would have been lost forever but for her

protectors who recorded it and kept a chronology of her descendants. In the fifth century, Magdalene line intermarried with French royalty and created a lineage of Merovingian bloodline. The church now wanted to destroy all records that told her true story. These documents were secretly stashed beneath the ruins of Herod's temple in Jerusalem. Texts written by Christ and bone of Magdalene, too, were buried there.

It is believed that the crusaders' chief goal was to liberate the Holy Land, which is not true. Their chief goal was to find and destroy these documents. Some truth-honouring warriors, known as Knights Templar, thwarted this diabolical quest. A secret brotherhood called the Priory of Sion, formed in 1099 to protect and pass on the truth from generation to generation raised the Knights Templar. The French king Godfrey of Bouillon, himself of this bloodline, founded the Priory.

The knights at last found the precious documents in Jerusalem and gained considerable bargaining power with the Vatican. But in October 1307, Pope Clement V had all the Knights rounded up and killed after a conspiracy with King Philip IV of France. The stunning speed of execution eliminated most of the knights but the few who survived had the explosive documents. They were entrusted to members of the Priory who faithfully guarded the treasure over centuries, passing on only through codes and symbols — the most famous being the Holy Grail.

The Grail is not the cup that Jesus used during the Last Supper but a metaphor for Magdalene. The search for the Holy Grail means kneeling before the bones of Magdalene. The secret location of the Grail is known only to the Priory (and to Dan Brown, of course). Leonardo da Vinci, Sir Isaac Newton, the Italian painter Botticelli, Victor Hugo and many other famous persona were called the Grand Masters of the Priory. Through three famous paintings ('Mona Lisa', the 'Last Supper' and 'Virgin of the Rocks') Leonardo expresses his own worship of the sacred feminine and his disdain for Christianity.

* * *

Decoding The Da Vinci Code Lies   xxiii

Dan Brown has taken the cue from the book, *Holy Blood, Holy Grail*, by Michael Baigent, Richard Leigh, and Henry Lincoln, which was a best seller in the 1980s. Both begin with a mystery leading to more sinister intrigues. In *The Da Vinci Code*, it is the murder of a curator at the Louvre; in *Holy Blood, Holy Grail*, it is the affluence of a priest in a French village. When BBC documentary producer Henry Lincoln's mind was fired by the popular fiction writer Gerard de Sede's story of a priest who found parchments of coded messages and encashed them to become rich overnight, the stage was set for three bestsellers to come.

Lincoln now enlisted Baigent and Richard for research and who became co-authors of the book. They came out with a welter of names, dates and genealogies about a secret society called the Priory of Sion, founded in Jerusalem in 1099. This society is supposed to guard documents and proofs that Mary Magdalene was the wife of Jesus and that she carried his child with her when she fled to what is now France. Their descendants eventually founded the Merovingian dynasty of Frankish monarchs. Deposed in the eighth century, the Merovingian lineage still exists. And the Priory is awaiting the most auspicious moment to reveal the astonishing truth and reclaim the Holy Roman Empire.

In the **New York Times Book Review** (Feb 22, 2004), critic Laura Miller lambastes the book: "*Holy Blood, Holy Grail* is a masterpiece of insinuation and supposition, employing all techniques of pseudo-history to symphonic effect ... Dozens of credible details are heaped up in order to provide a legitimising cushion for rank nonsense.... The authors spin one gossamer strand of conjecture over another, forming a web dense enough to create the illusion of solidarity. Though bogus, it's an impressive piece of work."

Ironically, the legitimacy of the Priory rests on pseudonymous documents a man named Pierre Plantard planted in the Bibliotheque Nationale. Plantard's own confederates have admitted to fabricating materials, including genealogy, to show Plantard as a descendant of the Merovingians (of Jesus Christ).

Tampered, too, was the list of the Priory's "grand masters" — Botticelli, Isaac Newton, Jean Cocteau and, of course, Leonardo da Vinci — which Dan Brown trumpets under the heading 'Fact'.

Plantard finally turned out to be "an inveterate rascal with a criminal record". A series of French books have debunked the Plantard hoax and a BBC documentary in 1996 has exposed it. Interestingly, the actual Priory of Sion was a harmless group of like-minded friends formed in 1956.

* * *

The original story revolves around a young, educated priest, Berenger Sauniere, of St Mary Magdalene church in Rennes-le-Chateau, an isolated small town in southwest France. France went to the polls in 1885, the same year the priest assumed charge of this church. The major national debate then was should France return to a pro-Catholic monarchy or remain a republic. This young priest who is a fiery preacher supported the return to a pro-Catholic monarchy, and the Countess of Chambord, widow of the claimant to the throne, reportedly gave him 3,000 livres as a reward of his loyalty and to renovate his church. During the renovation of his dilapidated church, some coded parchments hidden in a hollow pillar were discovered. Sauniere took the parchments to Paris and showed them to experts. In the city, he befriended occultists and esoterics, among them Emma Calve, with whom he is reported to have an illicit affair.

Back in his home parish, the priest appears to have suddenly become rich. People were intrigued by his lavish lifestyle and ordering expensive books for his library. And they were dismayed when the priest embarked on a number of building projects, including the renovation of the ancient parish church, construction of a large house called Villa Bethania, and the Tour Magdala, which he used as his library. Rumours soon spread that hidden treasures were found in night excavations in and around his church.

The abbe Sauniere eventually lost his position because he was selling mass indulgences by mail all over Europe. That could explain how he became so wealthy. He died on January 22, 1917, leaving his house and tower to his lifelong housekeeper, Marie Denardaud — who, some say, was his mistress. Buried treasures somehow caught on the imagination of authors and documentary producers.

In another part of France, a small group of friends formed a recreational club called the Priory of Sion on June 25, 1956, in Annemasse, Haute-Savoie. The mountain Col du Mont Sion nearby seems to have influenced the name of the club. It was disbanded the next year, but had a politicised incarnation under Pierre Plantard. His mentor was an anti-Semitic utopian nationalist named Paul Le Cour. The Priory brought out periodicals called Circuit, which appeared on and off during the '50s and '60s.

To oppose the first Jewish prime minister of France, Leon Blum, and his leftist government, Plantard formed an association called The French Union in 1937. Another attempt to start a political organisation called French National Renewal in 1941 was foiled by the government. Plantard hobnobbed with a rightwing society of occult nationalism — the kind of which flourished during the Vichy regime (1940-41) but faded after 1942. In the early 1950s, Plantard served four months in Fresnes prison, convicted of fraud and embezzlement.

In the early 1960s, Plantard discovered his genius for forging documents meant to showcase him as a descendant of the Merovingian royal line and to win credibility for the Priory of Sion. His enterprising associates deposited fake documents in the Bibliotheque Nationale in Paris. In 1965 his henchman Philip de Cherisey fabricated parchments supposedly found by Berenger Sauniere in Rennes-le-Chateau. They also tampered with genealogical documents of the Merovingian kings and added famous personalities like Leonardo da Vinci, Isaac Newton and Jean Cocteau to the list of members of the Priory.

The next part of the hoax was to spin and disseminate the fairy tale. To this end, Plantard cleverly enlisted Gerard de Sede who published two books about the dossiers — one of which reproduced the two coded parchments found by by Berenger Sauniere and signed "PS," for Priory of Sion. Unfortunately, Plantard and De Sede had a fight over royalties and De Cherisey began telling everyone quietly that the parchments had been faked.

When an investigative journalist, Jean-Luc Chaumeil, published a story in 1973 calling the dossiers a hoax, historians and media persons began disputing other parts of the story. In 1974, historian Rene Descadeillas debunked the story of the treasure. But the British film producer, Henry Lincoln, did a series of three documentaries for BBC TV: The Lost Treasure of Jerusalem (1972), The Priest, the Painter and the Devil (1974), and The Shadow of the Templars (1979). Encouraged by the response, he followed it up by the book *Holy Blood, Holy Grail*. Finally, De Sede himself came out with a book, admitting the dossiers were forged and the Merovingian line does not exist today.

In 1997, BBC TV also produced another programme admitting that the story was not true. Way back in 1974, Rene Descadeillas in his book summed up the hoax thus:

"...They've tried to drag in emperors, kings, archdukes, princes, archbishops, the grandmasters of every conceivable Order, magi and alchemists, philosophers, historians, magistrates, and humble monks and priests ... they have brought into existence people whose existence is far from certain and have given birth to others who never existed in the first place. They've touted magicians, paraded mediums in front of us, conjured up spirits and interrogated clairvoyants. They've fabricated books of magic spells, family trees and wills, and have uncovered illegitimacies, murders and assassinations. They've lied to the point of absurdity and have even — surely the ultimate in ridiculousness — invoked the name of the Devil! "

* * *

"Everyone loves a good conspiracy. The secret societies in Ludlum, Le Carre, J R Rowling, J R R Rolkien and Dan Brown novels prove this point again and again. From one stunning secret to another, from one coded message to another, The Da Vinci thriller moves. Dan Brown seems to have learned a lesson or two from Ludlum, who starts his novels with a stunning secret, then throws a man — or a bewitchingly beautiful woman — into fast-paced actions; while he (she) tries to figure out the secret, often against an impending threat to human civilization, introduce secret societies that no one thought still existed, and in the break-neck speed the reader is overawed into believing in the cardboard characters."

* * *

Just 20 years after Loenardo painted the 'Last Supper', it was called a wreck, even during his lifetime. In the 16th century, it was called a faded smudge and was restored in 1726 and 1770. Hung in a room that Napoleon's troops used as barracks in 1799 and as a stable, it was damaged in a flood in 1800 and a door was cut through the bottom of it. And there was an attempt to remove it from the wall in 1821. It was restored in 1854-55, 1907-8, 1924, 1947-48, 1951-54 and throughout 1080s and 1990s.

Today there is not much of the original faces left to make any serious judgement. Christ's face is completely modern suggesting repainting. His hands are spread out on the table, the right hand reaching towards a piece of bread and the left hand reaching towards a cup of wine. And that's the hand that points down. Clearly, the institution of the Holy Eucharist through the bread and wine is in focus. But Brown expects the modern day chalice in the 'Last Supper' and the absence of which he finds an excuse to introduce Mary Magdalene into the picture.

Brown sees a disembodied hand that threatens Mary Magdalene and tries to suppress the feminine side of the church. Look carefully, it's the hand of Simon Peter signifying the premonition of his cutting the ear of the chief priest's servant on the arrest of Jesus. The beardless person sitting on the right of Christ is St John, the youngest disciple who in most paintings has a feminine appearance — a perfect feminine presentation of John could be seen in Raphael's Crucifixion (London National Gallery).

Coming to the painting 'Virgin of the Rocks', Brown argues that it is heretical because he confuses John the Baptist with Christ and vice-versa. It was a religious commission for the Confraternity of the Immaculate Conception for the church of San Francesco Grande in Milan, not for nuns as Brown says.

Artists dealing with the 'Last Supper', highlight one of the two aspects: the identification of the traitor or the institution of the Eucharist. What Leonardo does is portray the announcement, ``I am going to be betrayed,'' and the aftermath and the shock.

In this context, critic Diane Apostolos-Cappadona's comments merit our attention: "In the larger context of Leonardo's oeuvre, gestures are humanising as well as symbolic. In this particular painting, the gestures signify surprise, disbelief, accusation, and awe or wonder. This is what is important in this painting. The Jesus figure is set off in a particular way because the others are stunned. He is both the announcer and the betrayed."

"I do not believe there is a woman in the 'Last Supper' and I do not believe in any way that it's Mary Magdalene. I think that the V that's there — the one Dan Brown defines as a symbol of femininity — is there, first of all, to emphasise the Christ figure and to emphasise the reality of the perspective within that fresco."

Perspective is extraordinarily important in Renaissance art, especially in Leonardo's paintings. The apostles are all grouped into triangular formations. "Dan Brown has omitted any discussion of pyramidal composition in Leonardo's oeuvre, of the four triangular groupings which are important to form the compositional balance for the central triangular figure who is Jesus. Centrally positioned, Jesus is in a pyramidal posture, and it is this pyramidal composition that is one of Leonardo's great gift to Western art.

The 'Last Supper' was created on a wall, in a refectory where the monks ate. They either looked up at it or at the painting of the crucifixion on the opposite wall depending on …what meal it was, and what prayers were being recited. So the painting functioned differently, at different days of the liturgical calendar. Dan Brown ignores totally that original monastic context.

* * *

Damn lies, Dan Brown! To amass a fortune lying is a fiction writer's licence. Nevertheless, a million lies will not match the power of truth that is eternal.

Book One

THE WEBSITE OF GOD

Human thirst for blood is insatiable seen through history. And there stood a defining moment in the history of mankind when a frenzied mob was baying for the blood of a young rabbi who was an itinerant teacher like Socrates, Plato, or Aristotle.

Mad with rage the crowd yelled, "Crucify him, crucify him, crucify him."

"But he is innocent," declared the Roman governor from the judgement seat.

"We have a law that judges him guilty," shouted the crowd.

"Then I will slash him and free him," said the governor, hoping some cruelty would appease the crowd.

"If you free him you are an enemy of Caesar," roared the crowd. "This man claimed to be a king and we have no other king but Caesar."

Nervous and beaten at the very mention of Caesar, Pontius Pilate took water and washed his hands in public, and said, "I am innocent of his blood."

"Let his blood be upon us and our children," yelled the crowd. Now travel forward two millennia from Palestine under imperial Rome to Nazi Germany. Do you see Hitler's gas chamber and half a million Jews perishing in it? The story of the Jews since the cross has been a harrowing and tragic one, driven out of homeland and their temple razed to the ground, wandering with the cross of the albatross around the neck, homeless, stateless, witch-hunted, going from country to country... till the state of Israel was formed half a century ago.

Do you see no connection between the cross and the tragedy of the Jews? They thought it was all over on the Friday of April 30 AD. They neatly executed the Prophet of Nazareth who challenged their tradition and threatened their business interests. But it was only the beginning of their troubles as in three days some women and some of his disciples are reported to have seen him alive; and their number increased and in forty days some five hundred are reported to have seen him at once.

The Jewish leaders were at their wit's end when more and more people and even some of their most trusted leaders like Nicodemus and Joseph of Arimathea defected to the Way. That fisherman Peter gave a stirring sermon and three thousand Jews were gone after him. How could sensible people be so crazy as to believe that a dead man could come back to life and give them eternal life? And if he were in a coma and came back to consciousness, as some would like to doctor it, how can he deceive so many, some of whom are most educated and balanced of people?

Then came the worst tremor of all: one of their war-horses called Saul of Tarsus, who vigorously persecuted people of the New Way as they were called, defected. The Prophet of Nazareth seems more powerful in his death than in his life. The story of Saul goes something like this: In his red-hot fury, Saul with his accolades went about persecuting the people of the New Way in Damascus when he saw a blinding light and he was thrown off the horse. Lying on the road, blind and helpless, he heard a voice, "Saul, Saul, why do you persecute me?", to which Paul said, "Who are you Lord?" "I am Jesus of Nazareth whom you persecute. Now get up and go to the city and there you will be told what you should do."

Blind and fasting Saul remained for three days incessantly praying when in the same city a man named Ananias had a vision.

Book One

"Go to the house of Judas and ask for a man from Tarsus named Saul..." Ananias was told. "But Lord, this man has come to persecute your people," protested Ananias. "Go! This man is my chosen instrument to carry my name before the gentiles and their kings and before the people of Israel...," Ananias was told.

Then we see Ananias in the house of Judas placing his hands on Saul and saying, "Brother Saul, Lord Jesus who appeared to you on the road as you were coming here has sent me so that you may see again and be filled with the Holy Spirit." Immediately something like scales fell from Saul's eyes and he could see again. He got up and was baptised and he took some food and regained strength.

Had Jesus Christ not risen from the dead, there would have been no Saint Paul; but in his place there would have been a bigot, killing, plotting and whipping up communal hatred in the name of God. There would sure have been no Pauline epistles exhorting, "Who shall separate us from the love of Christ? Shall trouble or hardship or persecution or famine or nakedness or danger or sword? ... or, five times I received from the Jews the forty lashes minus one, three times I was beaten with rods, once I was stoned, three times I was shipwrecked, I spent a night and a day in the open sea. I have been in danger from rivers, in danger from bandits, in danger from my own countrymen, in danger from gentiles, in danger in the city, in danger in the country, in danger at sea and in danger from false brothers..."

Then there would have been no Peter the Great Fisherman, whose powerful sermons convicted thousands to repentance and embrace the New Way. There would have been no Saint John, the Apostle of Love, either. No James the Martyr, no Thomas the sceptic-turned believer, no Matthew the legendary tax collector, no Andrew and Philip, no Bartholomew and James the Less. Their master took men of clay, transformed and empowered them as the architects of the New Kingdom and the New Way. In fact, the transformed lives of his disciples are the greatest proof of the resurrection of Jesus Christ.

Four distinct possibilities beckon those in search of an explanation for the story of resurrection: that his disciples stole the body and proclaimed he is risen; that his enemies stole the body and let his disciples proclaim that he was risen; that he indeed rose again; or that he was in coma and regained consciousness which the disciples mistook as resurrection.

Let us take the first possibility that his disciples came and stole the body. And what do they get in return for preaching that he rose again? Martyrdom. Do you tell a lie to get killed or save your life? Stealing the body cannot give the kind of conviction that Peter had, his words cutting into the hearts of three thousand Jews on the day of Pentecost and later another two thousand, adding to five thousand embracing the New Way. Even the most skilful liars cannot convict so many, and that too people who have been witnesses to the life and ministry of Jesus. Compare the cowardice with which Peter denied his Master on the night of his betrayal and the boldness with which Peter spoke after resurrection. Also compare the self-seeking, self-promoting, self-centred life of Peter and the other disciples to the Christ-seeking, Christ-promoting, Christ-centred life of them after resurrection. Of course, Judas Iscariot was a fish of another kettle, who finding his calculations going awry, committed suicide.

What if his enemies stole the body and the disciples 'foolishly' went about preaching their Master rose again? His enemies were hell-bent on destroying the New Way and the best way to destroy it was to produce the body of Jesus while his disciples proclaim his resurrection — — making it the biggest mockery of their time. Their inability to do so rules out the second possibility.

It is preposterous to suggest that a dead man could be in a coma, as did some vainglorious pseudo-intellectuals. Saint John records that a Roman soldier pierced the heart of Jesus with a spear to ensure that he was dead and out gushed blood and watery liquid signifying the agony and pain he went through before death. Jesus has just died when he was speared, otherwise his blood would have dried up. Since Pilate could not believe that a person could die on the cross so soon, he summoned the centurion to prevent any goof-ups. Meticulous as the Roman soldiers were, they broke the legs of the other two but saw Jesus was already dead; nevertheless, just to remove the last shadow of doubt, the Roman soldier went into swift operation, as if scripted by Destiny to prove to the world that Jesus of Nazareth was dead.

So we are left with the only possibility that Jesus Christ indeed rose again. The post-resurrection appearance of Jesus starkly differs from those in the days of his flesh and blood. The new body of Jesus could penetrate walls and closed doors, as he met the disciples in the closed room, closed for fear of the Jewish leaders. The new body could disappear and reappear as if from nowhere. It is a spiritual body beyond matter, space and time.

"That which we have heard, that which we have seen, that which we have looked upon and that which our hands have touched, that we declare unto you...," writes Saint John the beloved disciple at the beginning of his first epistle. And in his gospel, Saint John introduces Jesus thus: "In the beginning was the Word, and the Word was with God, and the Word was God." The Greek word Logos means the word, the reason, the will, the mind, the revelation. What Saint John is saying is that Jesus Christ is the Mind of God, the Will of God, the Reason of God, the Word of God, the Medium of God, the Message of God. To Saint Paul, Jesus Christ is the *pleuroma* or the *effulgence* or the fullness of God's glory. In other words, the fullness of Godhead dwelt in the person of Jesus Christ.

The theme of Saint John's gospel reads: "I write this so that you may believe, and by believing you may have eternal life." How does believing help is a legitimate question one would like to ask. Believing changes one's paradigms of life, gives a new outlook, sets new goals, embraces new values, appreciates goodness in others, values time, helps the less fortunate ones, imparts courage and wisdom especially in critical times. Believing is the pathway to a New Life and the beginning of the New Way.

Believing opens the door of heaven and grants access to the

unlimited power of the Spirit of God to realise your full potential. In believing, the finite meets the Infinite; the mortal meets the Immortal; the ephemeral meets the Eternal. In believing you embrace Eternal Life, or the fullness of Life, which is the very Life of God.

Believing shuns evil — pride, lust, greed, envy, malice, anger — and prepares one for the good life, whose main spring is God. By believing, one experiences the peace and joy that God gives which is quite unlike anything the world can give. The world is trapped in illusions and vanities, deceptions and self-deceptions that its inhabitants are unable to lift their eyes to the Truth. Like butterflies rushing to the fire for self-destruction, Homo sapiens rush to material gods to their eternal dissatisfaction.

Believing opens our eyes to the folly of acquisitions and disquieting avarice. It opens our eyes to the tragic consequences of an immoral life and the listless life of the ungodly. Believing opens new vistas of perception and avenues for excellence; it imparts a new dynamism to your planning, execution, and living. Believing makes life more meaningful and goal-oriented; more caring and sharing than self-centred. It teaches one to accomplish greater things and pursue nobler causes in life. It rewards life's endeavours with greater success because you realise the divine potential in you. In sum, believing is realising the godly spark in you; for you are created in the image of God.

THE WRATH OF HEROD

Ask anyone in Nazareth who is the best carpenter of the town. Everyone will point to this remarkable man renowned for his workmanship. His face radiated a rare joy at work and he served the rich and the poor with equal devotion. His neighbours called him Joseph the Righteous because he was truly righteous in word and deed. A meticulous observer of the Jewish Law he fasted twice a week and helped in his own way the orphans and the less fortunate of the town. Courteous and good-natured he was well spoken of by the people.

Long before dawn he was on his knees to commune with his Maker. Then he studied the Law most of which he knew by heart by constant reading and meditation. He treasured it in his heart because he believed it reflects the mind and will of his Maker. At work it spoke to him, inspired him and brought in the living presence of God.

His espoused wife Mary was heavy with child when he heard the proclamation of Augustus Caesar that all his subjects must be present at their hometown for a census. Bethlehem was a 5-day-long journey, which was hardly advisable for Mary in her present state of health. But to defy Caesar was unthinkable and go they must at any rate. Trusting God, which was the first principle of the family, the two set out knowing little what the future was in store for them.

Joseph would have secretly renounced his wife but for the dream. He knew it was God's plan that he must be the custodian of the Child she was to bear. He had passed through an ordeal by fire and came out victorious; his worldly sense whispered, 'It was utter nonsense, the palatable stuff of the gullible,' but the Spirit assured him the Child is to be a propitiation for the world.

Mary seldom ate without sharing her food with the poorest of her neighbours; she comforted the widows and orphans. Thrifty and hardworking, her countenance reflected the joy of a spirit-filled life. Joseph had seen her in prayer and at trance as though she was in the third heaven talking to angels and archangels and cherubim. While she lived on earth, she soared into the celestial with such ease and grace that only the spiritually awakened can accomplish.

Mary prayed for the liberation of her people through the promised King, the Messiah. Her people were once slaves in Egypt under the Pharaoh. They cried out to Jehovah who sent Moses to liberate His people. Forty years in the wilderness Moses taught them to be a nation. When Moses was gone came Joshua who led the people to victory and conquered the land of Canaan. Then came Samuel the Prophet who anointed King David after Israel's first king fell because of disobedience to God's word.

King David had extended the frontiers of his kingdom far and wide and established Israel as a mighty kingdom. His son Solomon built the first temple at Jerusalem and became renowned. But he married many women, daughters of the neighbouring gentile kings, and lost his devotion to the God of Israel who freed His people from bondage in the land of the Nile and provided them manna (bread) and water and meat of the fowl in the desert.

After Solomon the kingdom was rent into two, Judea and Israel. Idolatry reduced Israel to a province of Assyria while Judea lasted 150 years more only to be enslaved by Babylon. Prophets Isaiah, Jeremiah, and Daniel proclaimed the coming of the Great King of Israel whose kingdom will never end. The time of the advent of the Great King was at hand: on the streets, at the market place, at homes, at synagogues and the temple, and at Diaspora and wherever the people met they discussed the Messiah who is to come. Such was the expectation of the time that many virgins prayed they should be deemed worthy to be the mother of this Child.

Mary was in a reverie, thought of Abraham the Father of all Jews. Abraham rebelled against the idol-worshippers of his Chaldean city Ur and set out on a journey into the unknown. The idols have eyes but they don't see; they have ears but they don't hear; they have mouth but they don't speak; they have nostrils but they don't breathe; neither have they life; and those who trust in idols are like them — spiritually blind, deaf, dumb and without inner life — he concluded. It was then he was inspired by the living God to set out to the land flowing with milk and honey, the land he had not seen.

Human beings always find a paradise in the past and a paradise in the future; it is the present that is miserable. So there was a paradise in the Garden of Eden, the perfect setting for a human dwelling, living in harmony with nature and the jungle animals. There was peace and tranquillity all around, no one treading on another's domain. Then there was the forbidden apple and temptation — the temptation to take command of one's own destiny apart from the Creator. If life started with woman, temptation too must start with woman — the great temptress of man. And who must tempt woman but someone from that heartless species called man? So right at the dawn of human civilisation two ways opened up to Homo sapiens: living in unison with the Spirit of God and living by the carnal and emancipated flesh.

Time was when great teachers taught through parables treasured with immortal messages. Each understood according to his perception, interpreted according to his experience, and passed on to the next generation. Yet these parables radiate the same eternal truth through generations. The first principle the Garden of Eden proclaims is that behind the universe is a Creative Mind working out his design. The second principle is that Paradise is living in harmony with the Creator and his universe; and the third principle is that this Paradise is lost when the harmony or rhythm is lost.

Freedom has often taken humanity on the wrong track, at times returning to the right track. Civilisations have marched taking the right and wrong steps in succession; the Babylonian, Sumerian, Egyptian, Indus Valley, Persian, Chinese, Greek, and Roman civilisations have both flourished and decayed puzzling historians why history repeats itself. Then there was the twin city of Sodom and Gomorrah where horrifying abominations took place, and upon which fell the burning sulphur and fire of a crashing meteorite. And there were hideous giants with carnal appetite who polluted the human race in their burning lust but were flushed out from the face of the earth by the Great Floods.

God raised up great men at each crisis – Noah, Abraham, Samuel, David, Moses, Elijah, Isaiah, Daniel and so on. Whom would God raise up this time, Messiah the anointed king of Israel? Precisely then Mary felt a quiver of joy rising from her abdomen as her Baby moved within. "Hail, Mary, full of grace, the Lord is with you. Blessed are you among women..." She could remember what happened on that morning when she went in a trance while praying. She knew she would be remembered by future generations and that her Son would ascend the throne of David in whose lineage she and her espoused husband belong to.

What a difference between the spiritual world and the temporal world, the world of angels, archangels and cherubim and the world of Caesars and Herods and the Roman legion? She was perfectly at home in the former but a stranger in the latter. She knew the names of the seven archangels and how they looked like, having spent her childhood in the temple and overheard the exposition of the scriptures by learned rabbis.

The march of the Roman legions sends tremors down the spines of the people of Israel. The Romans rule the world by their military might and there is nothing a powerless vassal state like Israel can do. Ironically, such despondency breeds new hope, the very stuff on which marginalised societies exist. There were aristocratic and royal families praying that the supreme honour of conceiving the Messiah be theirs, knowing little that it had passed by them.

Book One

Bethlehem was five days' journey from the town of Nazareth where Joseph the carpenter made his abode. Nazareth was a thriving commercial city and a magnet for traders and craftsmen. Wages of course were low and so were the prices of essential goods. Luxury goods fetched a fortune because there were many who could afford them. Corruption flourished under Roman rule; offices could be bought and sold by which Roman officers became wealthy; and those who bribed their way up became extortionists and millstones round the neck of the ordinary folks. In their pursuit of luxurious living, imitating their Roman masters, the extortionists forgot all human values and became perfect torture machines.

There was no room in the inn for Mary's child to be born. She was already beginning to feel the travail at the end of their long journey even as Bethlehem came in sight of them. She beheld that princely city where the King of Kings would be born, as she recalled the scriptures: "Oh, Bethlehem Jaffratha, in thee shall....."

But no one in Bethlehem seems to pay any attention to this carpenter and his wife; innkeepers shooed him away because it was a busy season; they were looking for wealthy, comely, aristocratic people who would attract more such clientele. Poor Joseph and Mary made three detours of that small but neat town where Ruth once gleaned; its idyllic setting lent an ethereal charm to the town that is just three miles from Jerusalem. The southern Judeans did not pay much attention to the northern Galileans as they thought they were culturally and geographically superior because of proximity to the Holy City.

The carpenter was in real agony as Mary was in the throws of convulsions of pain. In Bethlehem nobody seems to understand, nobody seems to care, nobody seems to have a human heart: he has been going around entreating innkeeper after innkeeper sometimes the same innkeeper again and again hoping he would change his mind; but none did in the last two hours. When everything failed he thought he would kneel down and pray which he did.

As though touched by that gesture one innkeeper who shooed

him away twice beckoned him and told him he had a manger which the carpenter could hire for a week if he was that desperate. He seemed to be a pious Jew who kept his religion and business apart. Joseph heaved a sigh of relief and thanked God for His mercy.

People fast, pray and do all kinds of penance to reach God but God himself comes down to the humble and pure of heart. There were High Priests, Priests and Levites living in and around the Holy City but none was chosen to witness the birth of History's most famous child. Behold some faithful shepherds keeping watch over their flock felt a tremor and they saw angels descending and the sky filled with celestial light. There was heavenly chorus proclaiming, "We bring you good tidings of joy. To you is born a king in a manger in Bethlehem. Glory to God in the highest, peace on earth and goodwill towards men."

Startled the shepherds woke up. "Did you see a dream?" each asked the other. "Yes," they replied, each one to the next. "Did you hear angels singing?" "Yes," replied each to the next one. "Did you hear one of the angels saying, go to the manger and worship the Child?" "Yes," they sang in one chorus. "Come, let's see and worship the Child," one of them said and they all agreed.

The carpenter was amazed to hear the shepherd's story. Only hours before, he was pleading with innkeepers for shelter and lodging. Ignored by men but proclaimed by the angels, the Child arrived. Whom heaven honours, the world condemns, Joseph thought to himself.

Joseph, Mary and the shepherds, together, adored the Immanuel (God with us). Within they felt the transport of a joy they never knew before and stood still for how long they did not know. They knew what they saw is what the prophets prophesied centuries before; they knew what they saw is what Abraham longed to see but did not and what Moses longed to see but did not and what would have delighted King David most but could not see. This Lamb of God who came to take away the sin of the world is the desire of ages. Reverentially, the shepherds knelt down and worshipped Him, and disappeared as mysteriously as they came leaving a trail of memories behind.

On the eighth day the Child was brought to the temple at Jerusalem for dedication. There they met Anna, an elderly woman who spent most of her time in the temple, praying, meditating and awaiting the coming of the Messiah; and Simeon the prophet who was told by the Spirit that he will not see death till his eyes saw the Messiah. It is said that Simeon while copying the book of Isaiah stumbled on the verse that the virgin shall bring forth the Child. Simeon stopped at that and refused to move his hand. Simeon was expressly told he would not taste death till he saw the Child.

Simeon at once recognised the Messiah in Mary's hand, took Him into his hands and prayed, "Now that I have seen the Salvation of Israel, Lord, let me depart in peace." He told Mary, "A sword shall pierce your soul; for He has come for the rise and fall of many in Israel." He blessed the Child and departed; and so did Anna the prophetess.

There was a commotion in Herod's palace. Three men arrived on camel with gifts for the newborn who would be King of Kings; they said they want to worship the new king whose star they saw in the East. It was an unusually bright star in a strange planetary formation the kind of which they had never seen and it so intrigued them that they set out on a long journey to observe the phenomenon and to see the Child behind it.

Down the spine Herod felt a chill and he was mad with fury. So many he killed, even his own sons, to hold the scepter in his hand. His subjects, high and low, trembled at the very mention of his name. Every time a new emperor emerged in Rome, he defected to the winning side to keep his throne. Yet someone in his own kingdom dared to usurp his throne. The Old Fox Herod knew how to look unruffled and unperturbed even when a volcano was seething within.

Herod called the Chief Priests and the Scribes to find out what the scriptures say about the new king. The Messiah would be born in Bethlehem, they said. He directed the learned astronomers to Bethlehem; and pretending reverence said, "Come this way when you find Him so that I too may worship."

The star appeared to move before them till they reached the manger and then it stopped. There someone directed them to the innkeeper who in turn directed them to the manger. But the innkeeper simply could not believe that such sane people would travel all the way to see a carpenter's son. Too much learning sometimes produces eccentricity and he dismissed them as scholastic eccentrics.

Mary and Joseph were taken aback by the story of the magi and even more by the costly gifts of gold, frankincense and myrrh proclaiming His kingship, divinity and humanness. The magi had a long story to tell on how they spotted the star, travelled across perilous lands and deserts, came across different tongues and cultures and finally landed at Herod's Palace and the manger. To them it was the end of a long, long journey and the end of their search and research. The Infant was the climax of their Voyage of Discovery. In reverence they bowed before Him and offered their gifts. They departed leaving Mary and Joseph mystified.

Warned in a dream not to go back to Herod's palace, the wise men took another route; warned in a dream to flee to Egypt, Joseph and Mary fled the impending wrath of Herod. When he learned of the wise men's deception, an enraged Herod ordered the slaying of all infants under the age of two in his kingdom in the typical Herodian style. It was bloodbath in Judea and the wailing of mothers rent the air. Herod had only a few more months to live after that and worried that the people would rejoice over his death he ordered on his deathbed that 50 of the most reputed men be put to death so that the day of his death would not be one of rejoicing but of great mourning.

In his catalogue of crimes the slaughter of the innocents forms but a minor chapter. One of history's most blood-thirsty rulers, Herod ranks with Nero who is reported to have fiddled while Rome was burning and Hitler who in cold blood burnt half a million Jews in his gas chamber. The son of an Idumaean governor, Antipater, Herod makes his debut as the governor of Galilee at the age of 25 crushing a patriotic guerrilla warfare. Determination and cunning mark this man out who is ever looking for territories to conquer and people to rule. Timely defection, grabbing of opportunities and liquidation of rivals are the road he takes to drive himself power-mad.

For nearly a century and a half since the death of Alexander the Great, Palestine had been the battlefield of Egyptian and Syrian kings. When a great-grandson of Simon the Just, a renowned Jewish figure, bought from the Syrians the office of the High Priest he was inaugurating the corrupt era of Jewish high priesthood which was to continue through the time of Jesus. This High Priest adopted a heathen name and tried to introduce the Greek culture and language into Palestine.

The glorious uprising of the Maccabees under Judas who with an inferior band drove away the superior army of Antiochus Epiphanies who desecrated the temple of Jerusalem is part of the Jewish national memory. The Maccabees became King and High Priest but the decline of the house began with its success. Constant family feud, unmitigated worldliness, unbridled ambition and downright corruption brought decay and decadence to the Maccabees inviting foreign interference.

During the reign of the last Maccabees emerged Antipater, the governor of Idumaea who deliberately supported the weak Hyrcanus against his energetic brother Aristobulus. The sword of Pompey settled the dispute and Hyrcanus II was crowned king but the Idumaean governor became the virtual ruler and Hyrcanus II a mere puppet in his hands. When Julius Caesar defeated Pompey the prospects of Antipater and Hyrcanus appeared bleak, but by changing loyalties and helping Caesar in his Egyptian campaign Antipater was made the Procurator of Judea and his two sons, Phasaelus and Herod, governors of Jerusalem and Galilee.

The ruthless suppression of the guerrilla warfare won Herod

the favour of Rome but he was summoned by the Great Sanhedrin for the mass murder of Jews. There he appears in purple robes symbolically proclaiming himself king; and armed with the express direction of Rome for his acquittal; and had he not made a timely retreat he would have been slain in Jerusalem. Herod now returns with an army to settle his honour and was with great difficulty persuaded by his father to spare the city. And Caesar names him governor of Coelesyria.

With the assassination of Caesar, Antipater and Herod changed sides again; and they rendered substantial service to Cassius that they retained their titles. But Antipater was poisoned by a rival and the battle of Philippi placed the Roman world in the hands of Antony and Octavius. Once more the Idumaeans changed sides and Herod and his brother Phasaelus were named Tetrarchs of Judea.

When Antony was drained in the toils of Cleopatra, the Parthians entered the land to support the rival Maccabean prince Antigonus, the son of Aristobulus. By treachery, the Parthians take Phasaelus and Hyrcanus prisoner and Phasaelus kills himself by dashing out his brains against the prison walls while Hyrcanes was deprived of his ears making him unfit for the high priestly office. Herod flees to Arabia on way to Rome and succeeds with both Antony and Octavius and was proclaimed king of Judea by the Senate. A sacrifice on the Capitol and a banquet by Antony celebrated the accession of the new successor of David.

A king in title without the kingdom, Herod now raised an army and with the help of Rome marched on Palestine. It fell to the combined armies of Rome and Herod, and Jerusalem was under siege. Sure of the fall of the capital, Herod now turned his attention to the beautiful Maccabean princess Mariamme who was betrothed to him five years ago and marries her. Soon Jerusalem fell and terrible was the carnage. When the Roman army departed they took with them Antigonus and executed him to fulfil the wishes of Herod.

The first step of Herod was to execute forty-five of the noblest and the richest of Jerusalem for suspected loyalty to Antigonus. His next step was to appoint an obscure Babylonian to the high priesthood inviting the hostility of Alexandra, his wife's mother. Through her intrigues with Cleopatra and through the queen with Antony and through the entreaties of Mariamme, the only person whom Herod ever loved, Alexandra succeeds in getting her son Aristobulus appointed to the high priesthood at the age of seventeen. But when Herod saw the immense popularity of the young High Priest especially at the Feast of Tabernacles he was moved to murderous jealousy and got him drowned while bathing. And his mother denounced the murder and through her influence with Cleopatra who also hated Herod, the king was summoned before Antony. Bribing as usual got him out of trouble with Rome but troubles awaited him in his kingdom.

In his absence Herod had committed the government to his uncle Joseph who was also his brother-in-law by virtue of marrying his sister Salome. In mad jealousy Herod had directed that in case of his condemnation, Mariamme was to be killed because he could not bear the thought of someone else marrying his beautiful wife. Unfortunately, Joseph told Mariamme the truth just to show how much Herod lover her. On his return the infamous Salome accused her old husband of impropriety with Mariamme and when Herod learnt that his wife knew about the instruction to his uncle he was summoned and summarily executed without even a hearing.

To appease Cleopatra, Herod had to part with districts of Phoenice and Philistine and Jericho with its rich balsam plantations. When Octavian became the master of the Roman world after the battle of Actium and crowned Augustus Caesar, Herod had a new master to serve and present himself. This time Herod entrusted the charge of Mariamme to one Soemus with the same fatal direction which she learnt. This time not only Salome but also Herod's mother turned against Mariamme's protector who was slain without a hearing. And mad with jealousy Herod ordered the execution of the beautiful Mariamme after a mock trial. "The most fearful paroxysm of remorse, passion, and longing for his murdered wife now seized the tyrant, and brought him to the brink of the grave."

Alexandra, the mother of the slain Queen, deemed the moment most favourable for her plots but she was discovered and executed. Now in the Maccabean family there remained only distant relatives, like the Babas, who found asylum with Costobarus, the governor of Indumaea who married Salome after the death of her first husband Joseph. Tired of her second husband, too, as she was with the first, Salome denounced him; and soon he and the sons of Babas fell to Meredian intrigue. Thus the entire family of Maccabees perished.

Now the hand of the tyrant turned against his own family. Of his ten wives, Doris was the mother of Antipater, Mariamme, of Alexander and Aristobulus, Malthake the Samaritan woman, of Archa Archelaus and Herod Antipas, and Cleopatra of Jerusalem, of Philip. Mariamme's sons, Alexander and Aristobulus, were sent to Rome for their education while Antipater was sent into exile presumably to keep him out of succession.

Pleased with the services he had rendered, Rome rewarded Herod with the country east of Jordan, often called trans-Jordan, and his brother Pheroras made the Tetrarch of Peraea. On their return from Rome the young princes tied nuptial naughts; Alexander married a daughter of the King of Cappadocia while Aristobulus, his cousin Berenice, the daughter of Salome. You might imagine they lived happily ever after but that was not to be. In their Maccabean pride of descent the young princes offended his father's house which Herod initially overlooked. Salome could never extinguish her hatred of the dead Maccabean princes Mariamme or her sons notwithstanding the marriage; nor could the Maccabean siblings, Alexander and Aristobulus, disguise their feelings.

Finally Herod's suspicion began to be kindled against his sons by the constant denunciations of his sister and he recalled Antipater, son of Doris, from exile and sent him to Rome for education. Herod now took his two sons to Rome to formally accuse them of treason but the wise counsel of Augustus prevailed. The King of Cappadocia reconciled Herod with his sons for a while but the palace intrigues of Salome, Antipater and an infamous foreigner sealed the fate of Alexander and Aristobulus, who were strangled to death in a prison in Sameria where 30 years ago Herod married their mother Mariamme. Not just they who became victims of Herod's suspicions but 300 loyal soldiers who pleaded to stay the execution after a mock trial... they were cut down like sheep for slaughter!

Impatient, Antipater the heir-apparent, plotted against his father with the help of his uncle Pheroras, who was Herod's brother. On Pheroras' execution, Antipater withdrew to Rome but was lured to Palestine and was imprisoned and executed just five days before the death of Herod. "So long as he lived, no woman's honour was safe, no man's life secure," writes Alfred Edersheim in his book, **The Life and Times of Jesus the Messiah**. It was during this period that two of the greatest rabbis, Hillel and Shammai, lived and taught. Hillel was a Babylonian Jew who came to the capital to study at the Academics of Jerusalem, and eventually flowered into a great scholar who presided over the Sanhedrin, and possibly answered Herod's query 'where is the Messiah to be born?' with the prophetic answer, "In Bethelehem of Judea." Hillel is also the grandfather of Gamaliel, at whose feet sat Saul of Tarsus.

BEHOLD THE LAMB OF GOD

"Brood of vipers! ... flee from the wrath to come... bear fruits worthy of repentance... every tree which does not bear good fruit is cut down and thrown into the fire."

Neither his message nor his appearance was comely. Yet the masses thronged around this weird-looking man in camel hair, with long beard and unkempt hair, straddling a leather belt, who appeared in trans-Jordan. He lived on locust roots and wild honey and his companions were the wild animals of the desert. To the fashion-savvy city dwellers, he might have looked like a Stone Age man.

For 400 years Israel had not heard the voice of a Prophet. His message was simple: Repent, the Kingdom of God is at hand. 'But why repent? What wrong have we done?' you might ask. Repentance is an about-turn from a life of vanity to the reality of God, from being merely a citizen of the world to becoming a citizen of the kingdom, which has ethical and moral standards to keep.

"What shall we do?" they asked him. "He who has two tunics, let him give one to the one who has not." Caring and sharing is the cardinal principle of the kingdom of God. It lends meaning to your home, happiness to society, and greatness to nations.

He told tax collectors to be fair and soldiers not to oppress, which is righteousness at the workplace. So great was the expectation of the Messiah that they asked him, 'Are you the Christ?'

'No,' he said.

'Are you prophet Elijah?"

'No,' he said.

'Are you one of the prophets?'

'No,' he said.

'Then why baptise?'

"I baptise you in water but after me comes someone who will baptise you in the Holy Spirit and fire." His deep humility shone itself when he added: "Whose sandals I am unworthy to unloose." The baptism of John was the baptism of repentance but the baptism of Christ is the baptism (bath) in the Holy Spirit (the Spirit of God) and in the purifying fire that cleanses the human spirit to sparkle.

It may be recalled that John the Baptist's father, Zachariah the Priest, had a vision while he was offering the incense at the Temple of Jerusalem, where Gabriel the Archangel appeared and told him he would have a son whom he should call John. Cynicism got the better of the old Priest who was chastised for it and he remained dumb till the child was born and named John.

Then came the climax to John's ministry: before him stood someone who, the Spirit signified, is the Messiah. The two pair of eyes met, one in total disbelief and the other in a knowing smile. The Baptist was unable to speak for a while; regaining composure, he confessed he himself needed baptism by Jesus.

'Do it now to fulfil all righteousness,' Jesus told him and the baptism proceeded. As soon as Jesus came out of the water, John saw heaven opened and a dove descending upon Jesus; and there was a voice like thunder proclaiming, "This is my beloved Son in whom I am well pleased." The Spirit revealed to John that on whosoever the dove descended is the Son of God.

The public ministry of Jesus begins with a voice from heaven. The testimony of the Father and the Spirit and the witnessing of John the Baptist — — accompanied by word, water and fire in symbolism. Thus there were six witnesses and anyone in the crowd who stood by River Jordan could ascertain the truth.

Is there an evil empire trying to snuff out goodness from the universe? Is there a prince of evil controlling the demons of evil? Satan in the Christian theology is the personification of evil and the author of it. He is ever trying to subvert the peace and harmony in the cosmos, assailing the human mind to gain a foothold and use it in his grand scheme for an evil kingdom. The world slipping into a chaotic phase day by day, with the proliferation of evil and hatred, is an indication of invisible forces at play in the universe.

Straight from his baptism, Jesus went into the wilderness to fast for 40 days and to be alone with the Father because he was about to embark upon His Father's business. "Led by the Spirit, Jesus went into the desert to be tempted by the devil," writes St Luke, which is the other side of the picture. Jesus is in that lonely place to take the major decision of his ministry: how to present the kingdom of God to the people.

Inaugurating the kingdom of God is a direct challenge to the rule of Satan over this planet and he would oppose it with all his craftiness and machinations at his command. To confuse and create doubts in human mind is his favourite modus operandi; frightening men and women out of their wits is his special strategy; but if these do not work, he whips up opposition from all quarters; playing on human emotions, caprices, weaknesses or ambition is his time-tested stratagem; he has many more tricks and deceptions up his sleeve, which the modern world consider in vogue.

After 40 days of fasting and prayer, Jesus was faint and hungry beyond description and the white flat round stones of the desert appeared as bread. Satan's most opportune moment to intrude into the thought realm of the Son of Man with an innocuous suggestion: Turn those stones into bread. How concerned is the devil about your hunger and thirst!

On the surface of it turning those stones into bread and satisfying his hunger seems acceptable but in the deeper spiritual sense it is presenting the kingdom through loaves of bread and sure enough there would be a big crowd if not for the living bread the perishing one. That is precisely what the Son of Man does not want and he rejects it outright recognising its diabolic nature. Even at the personal level using his spiritual powers for satisfying his own hunger is not what the Messiah came into the world for and he quotes Scripture: "Man shall not live by bread alone, but by every word of God!"

The next moment he could visualise standing on a high mountain and seeing all the kingdoms of the world and their glory. Why not the kingdom of God be one such, the most powerful one making pygmies of the kingdoms of Alexander and Caesar? With magnificent palaces, broad avenues, and pomp and luxury such as the world has never seen? Then the power and comfort, and luxury will degenerate the kingdom and the lives of its citizens will become rotten. 'If you will worship me, all will be yours' reverberated the voice of the evil one. Once again, the Son of Man demolished the author of the thought quoting Scripture, "Get behind me, Satan! For it is written, You shall worship the Lord your God, and him only you shall serve."

In another moment he was on the pinnacle of the temple of Jerusalem. The temptation to do something spectacular and win the instant attention of the crowds assailed his mind. A celestial circus would draw the crowds to the kingdom but their commitment to God would remain suspect. The Son of Man drove away the evil one by quoting Scripture a third time, "You shall not tempt the Lord your God."

Satan makes his moves very subtly often assailing the thought process. First he suggests, 'If you are the Son of God, command this stone to become bread.' Then he offers, 'All this authority I will give you, and their glory; for this has been delivered to me, and I will give it to whomsoever I wish. Therefore, if you will worship before me, all will be yours.' And finally he himself quotes Scripture, 'If you are the Son of God throw yourself down from here. For it is written: He shall give his angels charge over you, To keep you, and in their hands they shall bear you up, Lest you dash your foot, against a stone'.

Twice did Satan attempt to create an element of doubt in the mind of the Son of Man with his phrase, 'If you are the Son of God'. In other words, `I challenge you to do the things I command and prove you are what you claim to be.' The Son of God does not need a testimonial from the devil and he always acts in his Father's will. But Satan is almost always successful in creating doubt in the human mind. `Does God really exist or is he a figment of imagination of the human mind? If God exists why do tragedies and calamities befall the human race?' Questions against the existence of God could be legion but consider the magnificent order and the fine precision with which galaxies move. A cosmic blast or an accident cannot create gigantic order but a Supreme Intelligence in command of the vast expanse of the universe — who is beyond matter, space and time. One has to be wilfully unreasonable to deny the existence of a Super-Intelligence often called God.

Doubting the existence of God is not the same as doubting one's own mission. Very subtly Satan is trying to create self-doubt in the mind of Jesus because he is human as well as divine — the perfect man and perfect God, according to Christine theology. But there is no space for Satan in the mind of Jesus and he is driven back beaten in his own game. Satan is in the business of scoffing at the things of God and destroying faith wherever he finds it. The next time you see someone laughing at the things of God, you can be pretty certain who is behind. God has granted him free will to be what he wants to be and to do what he wants to do till the end of ages when he will be cast into the Lake of Fire from where there is no escape.

Everyone who is ungodly is in the realm of Satan who has a claim over him; and adroitly he manipulates his mindset to see and believe the things he wants. The whole world lies under the domain of Satan because the majority of its inhabitants are ungodly; and that explains Satan's cheek to tell the Son of God, 'If you worship me, I will give you all these' (kingdoms and world powers). God worshipping Satan is abysmal blasphemy and the Son of God came to reclaim the lost human race and to make them sons and daughters of God — not by worshipping Satan but by defeating him in the spiritual battle. Make no mistake the demons have the power to make people rich and those who seek only material wealth end up worshipping them.

A craving to be admired and a longing to be worshipped lie deep in the bosom of every successful man. Satan is suggesting to the Son of God that he could do something like jumping from the pinnacle of the Jerusalem temple during the Passover feast where thousands of Jews would see and instantly recognise him as the Messiah — the shortest route to fame. But Christ's goal is to turn the people to the Father (God) and impart godly character to them and a divine circus is out of the question. In the temptations Satan presents a 3-fold strategy touching upon three primary areas of human endeavour — hunger, power and fame. In modern marketing parlance it may be termed a need-based, power-based and aspiration-based strategy which may have many takers but not the Son of God.

Jesus is now convinced there is no other way but the way of the cross to establish the kingdom of God. Just imagine, people who accept the kingdom of God are awarded $500 million each and appointed the CEO of a blue-chip company with palatial accommodation and fabulous entertainment allowance and an annual holiday in Switzerland. Then the whole world would be seeking the kingdom without genuine commitment to God's righteousness and holiness. The way of hardship, privation, humiliation and persecution will swift the chaff from the grain and the fair weather friends from the genuine ones. Indeed, in the end there is greater reward for seeking God than what the best of the world's plum jobs can offer.

The cross is the epitome of God's love. A love that embraces even the wretched of the earth, a love that conquers hatred, a love that inspires holiness, a love that imparts deeper meaning to life, and a love that death cannot contain and that lights every life.

The cross has a vertical dimension and a horizontal dimension. The vertical dimension denotes access to God by the cleansing power of the blood of the Lamb shed on Calvary. And the horizontal dimension denotes the fellowship and brotherhood of humanity. Without realising the horizontal dimension one cannot realise the vertical dimension, or a meaningful relationship with God is impossible without a meaningful relationship with one's own fellow human beings. As St. John succinctly puts it in his epistle, "He who cannot see his brother near him cannot see God who is invisible." At the end of the 40-day fast, Jesus is convinced the way of the cross is the only way to the kingdom of God and he returns to the Jordan where John was baptising with his disciples.

"Behold the Lamb of God who takes away the sin of the world," said John pointing to Jesus as he was passing by. Instantly, two of his disciples, John and Andrew, in quest of spiritual curiosity followed him. Jesus turns back and asks, "What do you seek?"

"Where do you stay?"

"Come and see."

In his excitement John notes the time he met Jesus: it was the 10th hour as the Jew would say or 4 pm Palestinian Standard Time (PST). The remaining hours of the day the two spent with Jesus and returned home rejoicing as never before.

Andrew could not suppress the joy in his heart and he told his brother he found the Messiah whom the Prophets wrote about. The two brothers now set out to meet Jesus and on seeing him Jesus says, "Simon, son of John, you will be called Cephas" which means rock or translated Peter. Looking beyond human frailties Jesus saw how Simon Peter could be transformed into a living stone to raise the edifice of the church, or to change the metaphor an architect of the kingdom.

The next day as Jesus was on his way to Galilee, Andrew

brought a man named Philip from his hometown Bethsaida. "Follow me," Jesus instantly tells Philip, knowing his commitment and serviceable disposition.

An excited Philip later brings Nathaniel (Bartholomew) to Jesus, telling him they have discovered the Messiah of the scriptures. Nathaniel was sceptical and asks, "Can something good come out of Nazareth," which means can a Prophet come out of Nazareth that does not ring scriptural bells as Jerusalem, Bethlehem, Carmel, Sinai and the like.

Philip has by now gained command of his Master's idiom and he uses it on Nathaniel, "Come and see." So they set out to see the Messiah.

On seeing Nathaniel, Jesus declared, "Behold an Israelite in whom there is no guile."

"How do you know me," insisted Nathaniel, kindled by the embers of his curiosity.

"Before Philip called you, I saw you under the fig tree," said Jesus to the utter amazement of Nathaniel. He was indeed under the fig tree meditating a scriptural portion, presumably a Messianic prophecy, and praying for the advent of the Messiah as many pious Jews of his time did.

Deeply convinced by the prescience of Jesus, Nathaniel confesses, "You are indeed the Messiah, the King of Israel."

"You believe because I told you I saw you under the fig tree. You shall see greater things than that. I tell you the truth, you shall see heaven open, and the angels of God ascending and descending on the Son of Man."

So Jesus becomes the magnet for his early disciples — John and Andrew, Philip and Bartholomew, Peter and James — assuming John did an Andrew bringing his own brother to Jesus.

A moment's reflection on John's testimony, "Behold the Lamb of God who takes away the sin of the world." Man cannot understand God unless God reveals himself. In the Old Testament, God reveals himself to Moses and through him to the people. Drawn to the miracle of the Burning Bush, Moses is commanded to put down the staff in his hand and it becomes a snake, the symbol of Satan in the Garden of Eden; and he is asked to pull the snake by its tail and it becomes a staff, the symbol of the shepherd or great leader. Then he is asked to put his hand on his chest and pull it out and his hand becomes as white as a leper's hand, symbolising sin in the human heart; and he is asked to put his hand back on the chest and pull it out and it becomes whole. He is again asked to pour a handful of water from the Nile to the bank and the water becomes blood red. These illustrations of the snake, the heart and the blood have deeper spiritual significance. The condition of the human heart is evil as if afflicted by moral leprosy through habitual sinning; and the reason is the snake and the remedy the sanctifying blood of the Lamb. John the Baptist testifies Jesus is that Lamb whose blood sanctifies the Inner Realm called heart.

THE WINE OF CANA

Ever since Adam met Eve in the Garden of Eden, millions of men and women have got entangled in the web — holy or unholy, legal or illicit, momentary or permanent, physical, or platonic — all of which cannot be called a marriage. But to the deeply religious Jew, marriage is a sacrament entered into by fasting and confessing sins. Jesus often uses marriage as a metaphor to illustrate man's union with God that lends a divine spark to human life and a super-consciousness that could be called the Seventh Sense. Marriage is the beginning of a new life analogous to the concept of the kingdom of God where purity and loyalty are the key to happiness.

Marriage is the merger of two identities to produce a new identity with one heart, one mind and one life in two bodies. But unsuccessful ones tell a different tale.

The oldest institution of humanity for fulfilment and security, it has survived many a tornado to reach our times. In the market-driven age, it has diverse brands: marriage for pure fun, marriage for family, marriage for convenience, marriage for professional value addition, marriage for upper mobility, marriage for money and marriage for divorce.

Today we remember the marriage at Cana not for the fame and fortune of the groom or for the beauty of the bride but for the most embarrassing moment in the life of an honest host — and the divine response to human insufficiency.

The modern village of Kefr Kenna, north-east of Nazareth, is considered the most probable site of Cana of Galilee. Nestled on the slope of a hill, it presents a picturesque setting with the rising terrace upon terrace of houses overlooking the large plain of Battauf. Beyond the hill is Mount Tabor and the Plain of Jezreel. Anyone driving through this smiling valley will come upon a fountain around which grows gardens and orchards that produce the best pomegranates in Palestine. Here was the home of Nathaniel Bartholomew the guileless Israelite.

The father of the groom may have learnt that Jesus is at Bartholomew's next door and walks across to invite him who now has gathered a few disciples. The hospitality of the host combined with his inexperience could be the cause of his momentary embarrassment. Some commentators say the host may not have made special provision for the disciples contributing to the crisis.

Betrothal in the Jewish custom precedes marriage by a period not exceeding a year, and at the betrothal the groom personally or by a deputy hands over to the bride a piece of money or letter expressly stating that the man thereby espoused the woman. From that moment both parties are regarded by law as actually married, except their living together.

A legal document fixed the dowry each brought and the mutual obligations and it closed with a festive meal. But not so in Galilee where people are more simple and pure, and eager to avoid anything that leads to sin.

On the eve of the marriage, the bride was led from her paternal home to her husband's. "First came the merry sounds of music; then they who distributed among the people wine and oil, and nuts among the children; next the bride, covered with bridal veil, her long hair flowing, surrounded by her companions, and led by `the friends of the bridegroom,' and `the children of the bride-chamber'.

"All around were in festive array; some carried torches, or lamps on poles; those nearest had myrtle-branches and chaplets of flowers. Everyone rose to salute the procession, or join it; and it was deemed almost a religious duty to break into praise of the beauty, the modesty or the virtues of the bride. Arrived at her new home, she was led to her husband." Thus describes Alfred Edersheim.

Then the groom will say, "I take her according to the Law of Moses and of Israel. This follows the crowning of the bride and the groom with garlands, after which they sign a legal instrument called Kethubah that set forth that the bridegroom honour, keep and care for her.

The marriage supper follows the ceremonial washing of hands and benediction with the cup being filled. The feast lasted sometimes more than one day, everyone in some way contributing to the rejoicing; and finally the friends of the bridegroom led the couple to the bridal chamber and bed.

Customs in Galilee and Judea differed in that the pure Galileans have done away with the friends of the bridegroom which led to gross impropriety; and all invited guests are called the children of the bride chamber.

The scene in Cana of Galilee: Amidst bridal music and jubilation the wine ran out, inviting shame and dishonour to the host. One discerning lady standing in the storehouse foresaw the embarrassment and sought her son's help as she always did in moments of crisis. "They are running out of wine," she said.

"Woman, what is it to you, and what is it to me? My hour has not yet come." Confident that her son would handle the situation, she told the servants standing by, "Whatever he tells you, do it."

There were six water pots of stone, containing 20 to 30 gallons apiece.

"Fill the water pots with water," he told them and they did. "Take it to the master of the feast," he said and they did.

When the feast master tasted the wine knowing little where it came from he said, "Every man at the beginning sets out the good wine, and when the guests have well drunk, then the inferior.

You have kept the good wine until now."

On reflection, the first question that comes to our mind is, Did Jesus show any disrespect to his mother? Did his words imply discourtesy or annoyance? The English translation 'Woman' sounds harsh but the Greek word 'Gune' denotes endearment and respect but is impersonal. Mary reposes faith and Jesus responds to her faith. But the word could be interpreted to highlight the new relationship after Jesus has embarked on his Father's business. Our possessive nature as father, mother, husband, wife, son, daughter would not so easily yield place to a new relationship. Mary must look upon Jesus as her saviour and learn to `lose her son' whose primary concern henceforth is the kingdom of God. This is in a sense a farewell scene to the warmth and comfort of life in the family before his taking up the life of hardship and sacrificial living of the kingdom.

A popular version of what Shelly wrote on the subject reads, "The water saw its Master and blushed." Jesus is demonstrating how the colourless, tasteless, odourless substance can be turned into a new substance — colourful, sweet-smelling, medicinal and that which gladdens the heart. This could be your story and my story. This transformation, in essence, is New Life.

Book Two

THE NEW LIFE

Flattery is the art of the Pharisee — who flatters to be flattered. One of the four sects that dominated the society of that time, the Pharisees claimed to be the perfect practitioners of the law while the Scribes claimed to be the perfect interpreters of the law. Sadducees did not believe in life after death while Herodians were a purely political party loyal to the house of Herod. Some Pharisees were Scribes as well staking double honour in society. The Pharisees did everything from fasting and praying to alms-giving only to be seen of men and esteemed highly. Men-pleasers of the worst kind, their true religion was hypocrisy. Nevertheless, honest men were to be found among them as an exception like the man who came to Jesus by night.

Nicodemus was one of the 70 elders of the Supreme Jewish Council called the Sanidhren that made rules and arbiter all temporal and religious matters of the community. So rich and privileged was he, yet he chose to come to this Galilean rabbi, who made a profound impression on him during the Passover at Jerusalem. The young rabbi had made a whip and drove away those selling inside the Temple declaring, "My father's house is a house of prayer and you have made it into a den of thieves." While people stood overawed by him because he healed the sick, he took the rabbis by surprise because he spoke in his own authority unlike they who quoted others to make a theological point.

Nicodemus chose the night to meet the rabbi because the night is the best time to study the law according to the Jewish tradition;

the night also gave him cover from undue publicity that the ruler of the Jews went in search of a still obscure Galilean rabbi; and the night unlike the day would be free of crowds that came to Jesus for hearing and healing.

The time he chose was perfect but Nicodemus was in for his first shock. Observe how Nicodemus greeted Jesus, "Rabbi, we know you are a teacher who has come from God. For no one could perform the miraculous signs you are doing if God were not with him."

Jesus did not return his encomiums but spoke sternly, 'I tell you the truth, no one can see the kingdom of God unless he is born again." Jesus looks at the heart and speaks to the heart because his kingdom is within.

It might have taken Nicodemus a few moments to regain his composure because his enormous wealth and prestige made little impact on Jesus. With Jesus' terse words still ringing in his ears came the second shock.

"I tell you the truth, no one can enter the kingdom of God unless he is born of water and the Spirit. Flesh gives birth to flesh, but the Spirit gives birth to Spirit." Astounding and unforgettable statements are characteristic of the teaching of Jesus, and Nicodemus was left wondering `how can a man be born when he is old, surely he cannot enter a second time into his mother's womb.' The religion of the Pharisee is external, made up of rituals and observances and nothing whatsoever of the inner realm. His carnal mind grappled with the spiritual realm but in vain. His desire to know the truth on the one hand and his lack of grasp on the other tore poor Nicodemus apart.

Born of water and the Spirit speaks in spiritual language of the New Life that Christ would give. Water is symbolic of the word of God that convicts, produces repentance, and cleanses the soul, which is the seat of the spirit. The natural man knows nothing of the things of God; but when convicted and cleansed by the Word, the Spirit of God takes over and guides him into eternal truths.

Even as water cleanses the outside, the Spirit cleanses the inside and plants the New Life, with faculties to experience God. A good man, a good Pharisee and a good teacher, Nicodemus was baffled. He found what he learnt, practised and taught so far crashed head on with what Jesus taught.

The New Life manifests itself by godly living and godly character, like holiness, love, peace, joy, compassion. In contrast, the life of the natural man is selfish, self-centred, self-willed, self-glorifying, self-seeking, vain, proud, unrighteous, adulterous, murderous, slanderous, culpable, wicked and ungodly. The natural man is heading for disaster because his propensities and inclinations are evil and begets only evil. That explains why the Planet of Homo sapiens is turning into a living hell.

"The wind blows wherever it pleases. You hear the sound, but you cannot tell wherever it comes from or where it is going. So it is with everyone born of the Spirit." Mysterious are the ways of the Spirit but you can experience his presence as the flutter of leaves in the wind though the wind itself is invisible. Likewise the kingdom of God is inherited by men and women inspired by the Spirit.

Now the discourse takes a deeper turn and come the third shock for Nicodemus: "Just as Moses lifted up the snake in the desert, so the Son of man must be lifted up, that everyone who believes in him may have eternal life." Only a short while ago Jesus told him, ``I have spoken to you of earthly things and you do not believe; how then will you believe if I speak of heavenly things?'' While Nicodemus was still groping for the truth, he heard the most profound statement of all, ``God so loved the world that he gave his only begotten Son that whosoever believes on him shall not perish but have eternal life.''

People reject God because of the evil welled up in their heart and they do not wish to be exposed standing near the holiness of God. Coming to God means rejecting evil and accepting His greatest gift of cleansing and transforming your life. "Light has come into the world but men loved darkness instead of light because their deeds were evil."

Nicodemus was not yet ready for the New Life Jesus is offering because he loved the praise of men more than the truth of God. However, three years later when he saw "the Son of man lifted up" on the cross, as in a flash of lightning he was spiritually illuminated. The words of Jesus reverberating in his ears, fear left him instantly and he was ready for the New Life. On that fateful day of history when Jesus' own disciples fled in fear, Nicodemus and his friend Joseph of Arimathia asked Pilate, the Roman governor, for the body of Jesus, and along with the Galilean women paid their last respects to the Son of Man, which we shall see in a later chapter. To be born again is to experience the creative and life-giving work of the Spirit of God. The Holy Spirit regenerates those who repent of their sins, so that they are adopted into the family of God. When a person is born again, he identifies himself with Christ and keeps away from sin; he spontaneously loves his fellow human beings; and keeps His commandments; and he overcomes worldliness and lives a godly life befitting the kingdom.

THE LIVING WATER

The quest for happiness is as old as man. Some turn to cigar and alcohol for happiness, some to sex and gambling. But lasting happiness eludes all till they find the living God. A much married Samaritan woman finds the meaning of life when she meets Jesus at a landmark well.

Jesus was on his way to Galilee passing through Samaria from Jerusalem. When the Jewish leaders came to know that Jesus was becoming more popular than John the Baptist as greater crowds came to him to be baptised by the disciples, Jesus tacitly withdrew himself from Judea not to provoke their jealousy at an early stage of his ministry.

The town was Sychar and the time around noon or the sixth hour as the Jew would say. Jesus arrived at Jacob's well, well known for travellers by foot; and precisely then came a Samaritan woman to draw water. The disciples had gone away to buy food and a weary and thirsty Jesus asks the Samaritan woman for water.

In dismay she turns to Jesus, "You, a Jew, ask a Samaritan woman for water!" The very term Samaritan was derogatory to the Jew because Samaritans were Jews who inter-married and lost their racial purity during the Assyrian conquest of their land and the Jews treated them as outcastes ever since.

A Jew is never seen talking to a woman in public even if the woman is his own wife and for a Jewish rabbi talking to plebeians is below his station. So Jesus broke the rabbinical norm, the Jewish norm and the gender norm all at once to earn the epithet the triple norms-breaker.

"If only you knew the gift of God and who it is that asks you for water, you would have asked him and he would have given you living water." Jesus is demonstrating how to engage a spiritual dialogue.

The metaphor Living Water has already caught on her imagination dwelling as she did in the desert ambiance. She takes him literally and wonders how he can provide living water without even a bucket. And she bluntly asks him, "Are you greater than Patriarch Jacob who gave us this well?" Jesus avoids an unfair comparison and takes the discourse further, "Everyone who drinks this water will be thirsty again, but whoever drinks the water I give him will never thirst. Indeed it will become a spring of water welling up to eternal life."

Beautiful thoughts come from beautiful minds and profound thoughts, from the depth of truth. And they are worth a life-time meditation, experience enriching it. The Water of Life that Jesus speaks about is the Spirit of God who imparts fuller knowledge of God, which is eternal life. Considering the enormous advantage of the living water, the woman asks Jesus to spare her daily grind.

This woman had come all the way to the well at noon when the sun beats upon the travellers on road most mercilessly – because of her low reputation. Yet Jesus deemed her fit for the kingdom if she would make a clean breast of her past and decide on a new life – a life of new ethics, new morals and new goals. To take the past out of her, Jesus said, "Call your husband." That was her grey area and the woman discreetly replied, "I have no husband." To bring home the need to change her immoral lifestyle, Jesus said, "You are right, you had five husbands; the man you have now is not your husband." Having no pretense to morality, she accepts Jesus' conviction gracefully.

"Sir, I can see that you are a prophet. Our fathers worshipped in this mountain, but you Jews claim that we must worship in

Jerusalem."

This woman of loose morals now becomes a seeker after truth, which moves Jesus to make the greatest statement on worship. "God is spirit and those who worship him must worship him in spirit and in truth." Worship springs from the depth of truth and true worship, from the depth of the innermost being.

Reflecting the hope of the time she replies, "When the Messiah comes he will explain everything to us."

"The one who is talking to you is the Messiah," said Jesus and that very moment came the disciples, as if enacting a divine script.

The disciples were astonished that their teacher was talking to a woman of apparently dubious character. The blessedness of the kingdom of God is open to the most wretched human being while it is closed to the 'holiest' hypocrite. God reveals himself to the humblest and the penitent and hides his face from the proudest and the stonyhearted. For the disciples, every day is a learning experience and when they brought him bread he replied to their surprise: "I have food to eat that you know nothing about... my food is to do the will of him who sent me and to complete his work." The life and ministry of Jesus revolves around doing the will of his Father and apart from that he had no desire or will of his own. His will is his Father's will always, in heaven and on earth. His strength, power, and joy came from doing his Father's will — a perfect model for a fruit-bearing ministry.

The woman in her newfound joy left the jar of water at the well, went to the town and told everyone, "Come and see a man who said whatever I did." The town was agog with the news that a prophet had arrived. Many believed the testimony of the woman but two days later they told her, "We now believe not because of your testimony but because we have seen the Messiah and heard him ourself." The people wanted Jesus to stay on in their town but he needed to preach in other towns as well and so he took leave of them on the third day.

In Galilee, the people gladly welcomed him because they saw the miracles he performed in Jerusalem during the Passover feast. At Cana where he performed his first miracle, a high-ranking Roman official urged him to go with him to Capernaum and heal his son who was at the point of death. "Go, your son lives," said Jesus. The Roman official went home believing and found that his son was healed precisely the same hour Jesus spoke to him.

CAPERNAUM THE NEW HOME

Glowing in the spirit and fresh from his recent fasting stood Jesus in the synagogue of Nazareth, his hometown for 30 years. It was customary for rabbis to explain the meaning of a passage in depth displaying their erudition and awareness of contemporary realities. Rabbis were held in high esteem because they were interpreters of the oracle of God and each great rabbi added his own interpretation; and as time passed by these interpretations became more important that the word of God itself.

This young Nazarene, tall and graceful with flowing beard and unkempt hair, had a mystique charm that spellbound the audience. The Nazarenes vow not to let the razor touch their head or beard. His sparkling eyes, serene countenance and gentle but distinct voice reverberating in the hall lent a divine ambience to the synagogue. And it was difficult for the audience to take their eyes off him while he spoke.

He was given the scroll of Isaiah to read and abruptly he stopped in the middle of a sentence and returned the scroll. All eyes were fastened on him. He read: "The Spirit of the Lord is upon me, because he has anointed me to preach the gospel to the poor; he has sent me to heal the brokenhearted, to preach deliverance to the captives, and recovering of sight to the blind, to set at liberty them that are bruised, to preach the acceptable year of the Lord...."

He did not read "...and to proclaim the day of the vengeance of our God"; or the rest of the passage in Isaiah (Chapter 61). In a drama of suspense the synagogue fastened its eyes on the young rabbi as if he was going to make a proclamation. "Today, before your very eyes, this prophecy is fulfilled," he said and sat down.

The synagogue sat lightning struck. Blasphemy, thought some: this son of a carpenter is claiming to be the central person of the Scriptures, the King of Israel and the anointed one of God to save his people!

His mother, brothers and sisters all they know; but when the Messiah manifests himself they will not know where is he from. Flesh of their flesh and blood of their blood, he could not be looked upon by his own town folks as the anointed One. Since they knew him from his childhood and he grew up among them, there was no way they could overnight think of him differently.

Jesus shot his words into the very heart of his audience pricking their conscience. It was their heart he sought to cleanse, change and make an abode of God. The heart, in biblical parlance, is the seat of personality or the core of one's being. It is in the heart that hatred, guile, envy, pride, lust, boastfulness, covetousness, and a myriad of human emotions originate and lurk in leading men to sin. For every clean heart there are a hundred unclean hearts; for every believing heart there are a hundred unbelieving hearts, for every receptive heart there are a hundred stony hearts. His message is always for the heart: to make it respond to God's word, even taring apart their prejudices so that they see the truth of God.

The young rabbi pricked them to rage. His audience believed the Jewish people were the most favoured of God and the rest of humanity were outcast. He exposed the myth by showing from the Scriptures how non-Jewish persons were at times preferred over the Jews — Prophet Elijah was sent to bless a widow in Sidon during the famine and Prophet Elisha healed Naaman the Syrian of his leprosy. No prophet is without honour except in his own town, he said.

The synagogue could take it no more. Filled with wrath, they rose to a person and thrust him out of the town. They would have cast him headlong from the brow of the hill upon which the city was built. But, miraculously, he walked through the crowd, down the hill to the city of Capernaum, perched beside the Lake of Galilee, a thriving city of tradesmen and fishermen, destined to be home to the Galilean prophet.

On the next Sabbath Jesus went to the synagogue at Capernaum. There he was greeted by a man possessed by evil spirits who yelled, "Jesus of Nazareth, have you come to destroy us, you holy one of God?" "Be quiet," said Jesus sternly. "Come out of the man." The man fell flat. When he got up he was calm like a lamb and Capernaum marvelled.

Simon Peter had a home in the town to which Jesus went straight from the synagogue. He healed Simon's mother-in-law who was sick and instantly she was ready to set the table. The abode of Jesus could easily turn into a public place where the sick and the troubled at heart sought his healing touch all the time. Poor Simon had to get used to staying in a public place even if that was his home. And his home became the most well known address of the town since it was virtually the headquarters of Jesus and his disciples.

THE LAKE OF GALILEE

The magnificent Lake of Galilee is an undulating witness to many touching moments in the ministry of Jesus Christ. It was on this shore that some of the prized sermons of Jesus were delivered; again it was on this shore that four fishermen forsook everything to become his disciples; on this waters Simon Peter walked imitating his Master; on this waters the faith of the disciples was tested by a tempest and this very waters Jesus rebuked and becalmed; on this shore the Resurrected Jesus served them broiled fish; on this shore Jesus recommissioned Simon thrice to undo his three-fold denials. The Lake of Galilee, proudly called the Sea of Galilee, is an emotional and integral part of the lives of the disciples.

It was here on a memorable dawn that four fishermen stood repairing their nets after a whole night's toil. Disappointment was writ large on their faces as they were planning their homeward journey accepting defeat. It was then the young rabbi of Nazareth walked into their boats and requested them to move the boats a little away from the shore because the multitudes were pressing on him. Jesus spoke to the crowd for a while and let them go.

And he turned to the fishermen and asked them to cast their nets on the right. These seasoned fishermen need no guidelines on fishing and surely you would invite their scoff or angry outbursts if you should offer them advice. Swallowing their pride they honoured the young rabbi and cast their nets on the right. Behold it was a miraculous catch and the net was about to break. They beckoned other fishermen to help because so great was the catch.

Overawed by a sense of the divine presence Peter confessed, "Leave me, Lord; I am a sinner." He said this on his own behalf and probably on behalf of those perplexed fishermen who found themselves tongue-tied.

"Don't be afraid, Simon," Jesus assured him, "from now on you will be fishers of men." Life will never be the same again for Peter and the other three who saw face to face divinity and they decided to follow him leaving everything behind. That was the new dawn in the lives of the four fishermen, Peter, Andrew James and John.

In another town, a leper fell down at Jesus' feet and said, "Lord, if you are willing you can make me clean." Jesus replied, "I am willing; be clean." Instantly the man was cured and he was told to show himself to the priests to attest his healing so that he remained an outcaste no more.

Jesus travelled throughout Galilee preaching and healing and his fame went ahead of him. Back in Capernaum while he was teaching in the home of a devoted man, four men climbed the roof and lowered a paralytic since they were unable to enter the house that was packed with people. Faith like this has never failed to touch the heart of Jesus — faith in the power and sovereignty of God.

God created man not for a sickly and morbid existence but for a happy and holy state of life. Sickness has its roots in mankind infringing upon God's spiritual laws. Germs and viruses or physiological disorders could cause sickness. That morality has a bearing on health is a lesson that Christ wishes to emphasise. Of course, branding every sick person as a sinner is wide of the teaching of Christ.

To the dismay of the Pharisees and Scribes, Jesus told the paralytic man, "Your sins are forgiven."

'Blasphemy,' they thought. 'How can anyone forgive sins but God? Is he saying he is God and we must worship him?'

Jesus divined their thought and said, "Which is easier to command obedience, `Your sins are forgiven' or `Get up and walk'." And he turned to the paralytic man and said, "Take up thy bed and walk" to demonstrate his authority over sickness which proves his right to forgive sins as the Son of God. Instantly, the paralytic got up and walked carrying the bed to the marvel of everyone around.

Tax collectors were synonymous with greed in those days. In the absence of a code of conduct, the tax collectors degenerated into extortionists doubly hated by the Jews because besides fleecing money they collaborated with the imperial Roman government whose yoke Israel longed to break. While robbers were looked upon as outlaws, tax collectors were a law into themselves.

On this Galilean shore, Levy the tax collector met a pair of eyes that melted his mercenary heart.

A seasoned extortionist, Matthew Levy never thought he could be a decent human being once again. Already he is experiencing a pull in his heart even as he decided to renounce his bad old ways and follow the Master wherever he leads him. Repentance brought him peace and showers of joy that he had never known. Matthew longed to share this newfound joy with his fellow tax collectors and so he invited them to a feast in the presence of Jesus. The 'indiscreet' act of Jesus infuriated the Scribes and the Pharisees who thought he was one of them, preferring their company to men and women of low repute.

"It is the sick who need a doctor, not the healthy," Jesus said extending his mission to the wretched of the earth, who too are God's children. Had Jesus joined the Pharisees and Scribes, he would have had the best of honour, the best of comfort, the best of food, the best of bungalows, and the best of life. But Jesus came to establish not the kingdom of man but the kingdom of God.

John's disciples fasted and even the Pharisees fasted twice a week. But not Jesus' disciples and that intrigued John's disciples. No one fasts in happy times like wedding but the bride will fast when the groom is away, said Jesus, implying his disciples cannot fast when he is with them. What John's disciples failed to understand is that while John lives in the old dispensation and Jesus is the new dispensation. No one joins a new piece of cloth with old which will tear away; nor does anyone pour new wine into an old wineskin which will burst. The kingdom of God, the new dispensation, needs a new mindset and new value systems.

IN JERUSALEM

Every Jew is duty-bound to present himself at the temple thrice a year: once for the Passover, once for the feast of Tabernacle and once for the feast of Dedication. For the Passover, Jews the world over converged at Jerusalem, the religious capital; the prosperous Diaspora brought with them icons of their prosperity; and business flourished in festival time around the temple, the chief beneficiaries of which were the chief priests themselves.

Not every Jew was religious, not every Jew prosperous, not every Jew at the pink of his health. In the festive crowd was a man who had a hunch back for 38 years. He had given up all hopes of getting well because every time he jumped into the Pool of Bethesda someone else did before him. The popular belief had it that whoever jumped into the pool first when the mineral water was astir got healed of whatever diseases.

Hovering around the pool were the desperadoes of society awaiting their hour of healing — the lepers, the blind, the lame, the maimed. Jesus who had gone to Jerusalem for the feast of Tabernacle was looking for the most desperate human soul. The choice fell on this invalid. "Do you want to get well?" Jesus asked in a voice ringing with compassion. "Sir, I have none to help me," replied the man characteristic of the kind of people Jesus seeks to help.

"Take up thy bed and walk," commanded Jesus and the man was amazed. He made an attempt to stand up and to his great delight succeeded; with ease and grace he walked through the crowd, of course, carrying his bed. This broke the Sabbath as neither healing nor carrying one's bed was permitted on the day since they constituted work. Jesus' motive was to unmask the inhuman face of the law as interpreted by the Jewish brass. Healing an invalid for 38 years is indeed an occasion for rejoicing and thanksgiving but not for the doctors of the law.

The Scribes and the Pharisees of Jerusalem took objection to the man carrying his bed in the precinct of the Temple, but he was unwilling to relent. "He who healed me said so," declared the man. Now they wanted to know who healed him as if there were healers dime a dozen in the capital; they already knew it was the handiwork of the Galilean rabbi whom they began to fear as every act of his threatened their authority.

Yet the man did not know who healed him till later in the day he heard a voice, "Sin no more, lest worst things happen to you." And instinctively he recognised that voice and ran to tell the Pharisees it was Jesus who healed him.

Their ire now turned from the healed to the healer. "My Father is always at his work to this very day and I too am working," he said gently. The reply enraged them all the more because he is now making himself equal to God.

"I tell you the truth, the son can do nothing by himself; he can do only what he sees his Father doing, because whatever the Father does the son also does. For the Father loves him and shows him all that he does." Jesus' exposition on the Father-Son relationship incensed them.

God is at the periphery of the Pharisaic religion. Their ingenuity in making sub laws to escape the rigours of the law is notorious while they imposed heavy burden on the people who found it impossible to keep the law without the craftiness of the Pharisees. The perfect hypocrisy of the leaders is only matched by a system that produced perfect spiritual blindness among the masses that only one phrase would aptly describe it all: the blind leading the blind.

"The son does everything that the Father does and has power

over life, to give life and to take life." They could not silence him because his works spoke louder than his words. Left to themselves they would have stoned him to death but for the fear of the people.

"For just as the Father raises the dead and gives them life, even so the son gives life to whom he is pleased to give it. Moreover the Father judges no one, but has entrusted all judgment to the son, that all may honour the son just as they honour the Father. He who does not honour the son does not honour the Father who sent him." Jesus reveals his divinity, the Judgement to come and the magnitude of their ungodliness.

"I tell you the truth, whoever hears my word and believes him who sent me has eternal life and will not be condemned, he has crossed over from death to life." The knowledge of God through faith transcends death and darkness.

"I tell you the truth, a time is coming and has now come when the dead will hear the voice of the Son of God and those who hear will live... Do not be amazed at this, for a time is coming when all those who are in their graves will hear his voice and come out — those who have done good will rise to live and those who have done evil will rise to be condemned."

Jesus leaves no one in doubt about his meaning and his authority. Cynics may scoff at the idea of life after death but eternal truths do not change just because they are not fashionable.

These words of Jesus illustrate the dual nature of his personality. While "The son can do nothing" statement reflects his human nature, "Those in the graves will hear the Son's voice" reflects his divine nature — both dwelling in perfect harmony in the person of Jesus Christ.

HOLINESS OF THE FOXES

The disciples of Jesus were hungry on a Sabbath morning and they started plucking corn from either side as they were walking through the field. The law permitted plucking and eating the corn if they were hungry but not on a Sabbath since plucking and husking constituted work forbidden on that day.

To understand the ludicrous absurdities of the pharisaic legal hair-splitting consider the following examples. Administering medicine to prevent the terminally ill from dying is not violation of the canon but in the process if he gets better it is a clear violation of the Sabbath. The demarcation of healing and prevention of death is a line like the equator that does not really exist but everyone is talking about. The catalogue of the tiniest objects that could be lifted from the floor is the ultimate in absurdity turning religion into non-particle physics, which you understand only when you are baffled by it. Travelling more than three miles on the Sabbath fell foul of the canons but the manipulators better known as doctors of law halted every three miles for a while and continued their journey unhindered. It was the holiness of the foxes that they perpetrated.

Gravely offended by the disciples' conduct, the Pharisees took the matter to Jesus. "Haven't you read in the scriptures what David and his men did on the Sabbath — they ate victuals that were to be eaten only by the priests and yet they remain blameless? Haven't you read in the law that the temple priests who work on the Sabbath remain blameless because of the holiness of the place?

Here is someone far greater than the temple (whose presence makes the disciples blameless), said Jesus to their irrefutable silence. Man is made not for the Sabbath but the Sabbath for man, he taught them.

Jesus and his disciples entered the synagogue where there was a man with a shriveled hand. Knowing pretty well his compassion for the sick, the Jewish leaders asked him, "Is it lawful to heal on the Sabbath?" "Who among you would not lift a sheep or a goat that has fallen into a pit on the Sabbath? To mute creatures, you show compassion; shouldn't you show greater compassion on man, made in the likeness of God?" Jesus commanded the man to stretch forth his shrivelled hand and he did to the fury of the Jewish leaders.

Book Three

THE ARCHITECTS OF THE KINGDOM

They were not the sort of men who came straight from Harvard or Princeton, Stanford or Oxford. They were not the sort of men who could be short-listed for a Nobel prize or Booker prize. They were not the sort of men whom Alexander or Caesar or Napoleon would have made a general in the Army. They were not the sort of men whom a multinational conglomerate would hire as legal luminaries or financial wizards. Neither were they media moguls like Rupert Murdoch nor gifted orators like Mark Antony. They came from the sea of obscurity with frailties and foibles. But the life of Christ electrified them.

The disciples whom Jesus chose to build the kingdom were mostly fishermen, known for their courage, enterprise and hard work. Ideologically and temperamentally, they were a mixed bag. Simon the Zealot could be called Simon the Terrorist in the modern parlance because he believed in bloodbath to liberate Israel. Matthew the Tax collector could earn the sobriquet Matthew the Squeezer because he squeezed every penny out of his own people to pay the Romans. Had the two met outside the influence of Jesus, Simon would have been at the throat of Matthew. The guileless Nathaniel and the crafty Judas are poles apart in their vision of the kingdom.

One suspects Simon Peter speaks faster than he thinks and indeed speaks faster than the other disciples. The Great Peter Principle seems to revolve around the axiom 'Be faster and smarter to succeed'. A split second can make or mar a fisherman as his prize catch could slip out of his net just the same time. The very epitome of Action man, the Hamletian phrase 'To be or not to be' never existed in Peter's Dictionary. The best of commendations and the worst of rebukes are reserved for Simon as if he gets either 100 out of 100 or a big zero but never in between.

Peter gives his heart and soul to the cause he believes in and easily becomes the spokesman of his group. He alone speaks more than what the other disciples have done together in the gospel accounts. Simon is indeed brave and demonstrates it by trying to protect Jesus and his men at Gethsemane but his courage deserts him when the housemaid of the high priest identifies him as a Galilean. He climbs the spiritual pinnacle at the Mount of Transfiguration but falls into the abyss by his infamous denial of the Lord three times.

Transparent honesty and generous disposition made Peter a cut above the ordinary. Peter's home in Capernaum in all probability could have been the headquarters of the ministry of Jesus who owned nothing in this world. If Peter's life abounds in contrasts, a study of his earlier brash, boastful, impetuous life and his transformed life after the day of Pentecost will prove rewarding.

Andrew Peter leaves all the talking and bravado to his brother and busies himself with taking people to Christ and his first fruit was his own brother Simon. Andrew is in the more soul-satisfying ministry of Personal Evangelism and has depth of character. An introvert he has a mind of his own that at times drives his brother Simon nuts and once provoked him to ask Jesus how many times should one forgive one's brother. During the Passion Week, certain Greeks come to Philip and Philip takes them to Andrew. Andrew, true to his nature, takes them to Jesus. With all his blemishes, Andrew is indeed a lovable person.

If brothers Simon and Andrew are cast in different moulds, James and John are so to speak Siamese twins temperamentally. Jesus calls them 'Sons of Thunder' and aptly so considering how they ask the Lord to bring fire from heaven upon the Samaritans who blocked their way to Jerusalem. James becomes the first among the Apostles to be martyred because the Jewish leaders deemed this man of sturdy physique and bold character far more dangerous than Peter the Great Fisherman. The surviving 'Son of Thunder' matures and mellows down into an Apostle of Love and the finest theologian of Christendom who peers into the mysteries of God as no one else could.

Philip could ideally fit into a Wharton School of Management programme; shrewd and calculating he could tell you how many dinari you need to feed a crowd of 5000 — or 15,000 including women and children. With his mathematical mind and flair for cracking numbers, he would respond to any challenge in permutations and combinations but spirituality seems his second nature.

Bartholomew also called Nathaniel belongs to that rare and disappearing species called 'honest men'. Meditating on the Scriptures is his first love that sharpens his antenna on the advent of the Messiah whom he almost stumbles on. Nothing indiscreet he ever says or does; yet he could be lost in a crowd of disciples and distinct on the dais for his sangfroid.

At the murkiest hour, Thomas prefers to brood over in his own company rather than fellowship with other disciples. On that fateful Friday when their hope died in ignominy and shame on a cross, Thomas sought time to adjust to the new reality of life without Christ. His scientific temper discounts the fiction of resurrection and demands seeing with his own eyes, touching with his own hands and probing with his own fingers before he can believe — that his Master rose from the dead. Earlier, when Jesus announced he was going to Jerusalem, Thomas responded, "Let us also go and die with him" - reflecting a streak of pessimism. Nevertheless an encounter with the resurrected Christ put him back on track and he utters the most famous Apostolic prayer, "My Lord and My God."

Unlike Peter and Andrew, James and John, and Bartholomew,

Matthew the Levi was not born into an orthodox Jewish family notwithstanding his surname. His early childhood may have seen demeaning poverty which he sought to escape by choosing a money-wise career. As he accumulates wealth, so does he the contempt and hatred of his own people. The day he met Jesus changed all that and his loving words still ring in his ears: "Follow Me."

The self-effacing humility of Matthew demonstrates itself in his gospel listing the names of Apostles: while in the other gospels Matthew precedes Thomas, in his own it is his companion who takes precedence. The Christendom is eternally grateful to Matthew for recording the sayings of Jesus with the penchant of a professional record-keeper.

The duo James and Thaddeus are almost anonymous; hardly anything could be said except that they were called. This James is designated the Son of Alphaeus not to be confused with James the Son of Zebedee. Today Jesus has many disciples of whom nothing could be said except that they are precious in his sight.

The last of the pairs, Simon the Zealot and Judas Iscariot, had things in common. Power had an intoxicating effect on both and both looked for a political kingdom. Judas was disillusioned when Jesus chose the way of the cross to establish the kingdom. Simon, who had sworn his last drop of blood to the Jewish kingdom before he met Jesus, succumbed to the love of Christ. In cold blood, Judas rejected it and took recourse to treachery and forfeited his soul.

The dualism of the Apostles is too striking to be glossed over: there are two Simons, two Jameses, two Judases (the surname of Thaddeus is Judas); two pairs of brothers Simon and Andrew, James and John.

Does the kingdom need a traitor? The kingdom of God is open to drunkards, harlots, traitors, hardened criminals, and even politicians — if they truly repent and receive the New Life. Judas squandered life's best opportunities by leading a double life; he went through baptism without repentance, he heard the greatest sermons without inner transformation, he witnessed miracles without acknowledging the deity of Christ. Judas's god was Mammon – the god of Money. His cup of bitterness was full when he was left out of the Mount of Transfiguration Jesus preferring Peter, James and John; and the preaching of the cross alienated Judas who was looking for the crown instead. The man from Kiriot might have cursed himself for being easily deluded by this Galilean rabbi who wrecked his brilliant career. The presence of Judas often brought squabbles among the disciples as he raised the question who is the greatest among them. Finally the kingdom of Judas crashed headlong with the kingdom of God crushing the Kiriothen to smithereens.

Jesus prayed all night before choosing his disciples as St. Luke tells us. He took men of clay and imparted them a heavenly vision and a heavenly character and spiritually empowered them to be the architects of the superhuman edifice of the kingdom.

THE SERMON ON THE MOUNT

On a hill in Galilee sat Jesus teaching his disciples when came the multitudes seeking the word of God. Instantaneously, the hill was turned into a platform for his immortal Sermon on the Mount that inspired generations for the last two millennia. It is generally observed that the quality of the audience determines the nature of the message, the quality of the speaker remaining constant.

Blessed are you poor: Yours is the kingdom of God. There was a pause, a mystifying pause that every renowned philosopher-teacher uses permitting the audience time to contemplate on the real import of the message. Clearly the obvious is not the intended meaning because the poverty Jesus is talking about is not physical but spiritual. Paraphrased, it reads true humility is the first step to the kingdom of God; pride, conceit, self-centredness and megalomania have no place in the kingdom. What is true humility but the deep realisation of one's own spiritual inadequacies to come up to God's expected standards often felt in divine presence.

Blessed are you who mourn: You shall be comforted. The pause allows the audience to look for the hidden meaning. Jesus is not suggesting that tragedy is better than comedy in real life or on the screen. The spiritually discerning watch over their words, deeds and thoughts, striving to follow standards of holiness, and repent when they err. The spirit of God consoles them because they belong to the kingdom.

Blessed are you the meek: You shall inherit the land. The land you inherit is the promised land, symbolically, Heaven. Meekness is not weakness but power contained. It is displaying bountiful patience in the face of provocation. Positive meekness returns goodness when tortured or harmed while passive meekness merely forgives. In short meekness is being Christ-like.

Blessed are you who seek righteousness: You shall be filled. He who seeks righteousness seeks God who is the fountain of righteousness (holiness); and he will not only find God but be filled with God and his ways.

Blessed are you the merciful: You shall obtain mercy. What you give will always come back to you in multiples. The one who finds goodness and mercy is the one who has given it to others. Give it to receive it is the golden rule.

Blessed are you the pure in heart: You shall see God. People who practise religion miss the essence for one simple reason: lack of the pure heart.

The atheist is too proud and self-centred to see the truth of God; the agnostic is overawed by uncertainties that anything certain becomes inferior to his intellect. The amoral finds his paradise in the lawlessness of the flesh that he cannot bear the thought of a moral universe; the existentialist believes nothing exists beyond his existentialism; and the scoffers find the old fable of God worth a hearty laugh. Yet the reality of God does not depend on the consensus of men and the purest of hearts experience His living presence as convincingly as what they see with their own eyes.

Blessed are you peacemakers: You shall be called the children of God. Peace is the presence of God in your heart manifested by a rare harmony within and without. A man who is at peace with himself is at peace with others while a man whose inner equilibrium is disturbed disturbs the equilibrium of society. The peace that Christ is talking about comes from the knowledge and certainty of God and does not depend on external circumstances which could be adverse. And with godly peace comes joy unspeakable — the hallmark of God's presence in your heart. Drug, alcohol and sensuality are mirages of the spiritual desert.

Blessed are you when you are persecuted for righteousness' sake: Yours is the Kingdom of God. The world cannot stand a righteous person because his life convicts them of their evil deeds. Facing martyrdom heroically is the supreme gift the righteous can offer to the extension of the kingdom. When your life is snuffed out your godly courage will awaken the seared conscience of the nation leading to a moral revival. The martyrdom of St. Stephen made a St. Paul and the martyrdom of hundreds upon hundreds turned pagan Rome to Christianity: the very garden of Nero where he burned Christians as human torches for his drunken party is the Vatican today.

Blessed are you when men shall revile you and say all manner of evil against you falsely for my sake. Rejoice and be exceedingly glad: For great is your reward in heaven; so persecuted they the prophets before you. Facing slander is one kind of martyrdom and facing persecution another kind that ranks you among the greatest in the kingdom, which is the triumph of your conviction.

You are the salt of the earth; but if the salt have lost its flavour wherewith can it be salted? Salt prevents decay and a pinch of it flavours the whole lump. One Helen Keller, one Florence Nightingale, one Father Damien, or one Mother Teresa can have greater impact on the character of the society than a million human beings who are mere statistics.

You are the light of the world. A city set on a hill cannot be hid. Neither do men light a candle and put it under a bushel but on a candlestick; and it gives light to all that are in the house. Let your light so shine before men that they may see your good works and glorify your Father in heaven.

Men and women of the kingdom constitute the city set on a hill drawing others to God. They are the beacons glowing in the goodness and holiness of God.

In short, the Beatitudes are the 8-fold principles for Christian living, or the 8 steps to the kingdom of God. New Life is manifested by character – humility, repentance, meekness, righteousness, mercy, purity, peace and joy even in the face of persecution – and character is the very foundation of civilisation.

Now Jesus gives a new interpretation of the law with a preface: "I have come not to destroy the law but to fulfil it. Heaven and earth may pass away but not a word from the Scriptures till everything is fulfilled."

Dictated by expediency the Pharisees divided the commandments into big and small ones, those which one can skip and those which one must observe, thus setting at naught God's commandments. So Jesus says: "And the least in the kingdom is the one who breaks one of the commandments of God and teach men so; and the greatest in the kingdom is the one who obeys and teaches men all the commandments of God."

"Except your righteousness exceed the righteousness of the Scribes and Pharisees, you shall in no way enter the kingdom of God." The religion of the Pharisee is self-righteousness, which is an abomination to God. Everyone who follows Jesus should set standards of righteousness far above those of the Pharisees who are downright hypocrites.

"You have heard Thou shall not kill but I say to you whoever is angry with his brother without reason is in danger of God's judgement." Hurting human life is a kind of murder that a child of God ought to keep away from. Should you call your brother a silly fellow, you are already in danger of judgement; and should you call your brother a fool, you are in danger of hell. Beware of offending fellow human beings created in the image of God.

"When you bring your gift to the altar of God and there you remember your brother has some grudge against you, leave thy gift before the altar and first make peace with your brother and then offer thy gift to God." An offering without love is an empty ritual; you cannot love God and hate man.

"You have heard Thou shall not commit adultery; but I say to you whoever looks on a woman with lustful eyes has committed adultery in his heart." Adultery begins in the heart and is expressed through the eyes before the act is committed; stop it at its origin. "Should your right eye cause you to sin, pluck it out; should your right hand cause you to sin, chop it off; it is better that you enter the kingdom without an unprofitable member of your body than condemned to hell." Holiness in the body is vital to dynamic Christian living. Unlike the Greek philosophers who taught the spirit is good but body (matter) is bad, Jesus teaches that the body is good and must be kept as the temple of God.

"You have heard whoever put away his wife shall give her a letter of divorce; but I say to you, you shall not divorce your wife at all, except for fornication, and whoever divorces his wife force her to commit adultery and whoever marries her commits adultery." Marriage is holy, so keep it holy. Adultery and divorce are anathema to godly living.

"You have heard Thou shall not swear falsely but perform thy oaths; but I say to you, you shall not swear at all, neither by Heaven which is God's throne, nor by earth which is his footstool, neither by Jerusalem which is the city of the Great King, nor by your head whose hair you cannot turn black or white." When words come from the depth of truth, there is no need for swearing at all.

"You have heard that it was said 'An eye for an eye and a tooth for a tooth'. But I tell you, Do not resist an evil person, If someone strikes you on the right cheek, turn to him the other also. And if someone wants to sue you and take your tunic, let him have your cloak as well. If someone forces you to go a mile, go with him two miles, Give to the one who asks you, and do not turn away from the one who wants to borrow from you."

Evil is real and living — and you face it everyday. Christ's answer to the age-old question how to conquer evil is through the strength of character and superior morals. 'An eye for an eye and a tooth for a tooth' is an exhortation not to kill a person for the sake of a tooth or an eye, or exterminate his family for the sake of a small injury. This is not a personal law for individuals to act upon but a social law for the government to enforce justice bringing home the idea that punishment should never exceed the offence.

Slapped on the right cheek and offering the left could be perilous dealing with the brute. But remember vengeance belongs to the sovereign God and God's mills grind slowly but finely in bringing poetic justice. This is personal ethics and does not apply to the realm of national security as some detractors have conspired to misunderstand. If someone walks off with your tunic after a litigation have the confidence to offer him your cloak as well because your God will provide for your needs. If Roman soldiers compel you to walk a mile carrying their luggage, which was common in those days, go happily with them two miles. If God has placed you comfortably in life and others look up to you for help do not turn them away: be a provider even as God is your provider.

"You have heard that it was said, 'Love your neighbor and hate your enemy'. But I tell you: 'Love your enemies and pray for those who persecute you, that you may be the sons of your Father in Heaven who causes the sun to rise on the evil and the good and sends rain on the righteous and the unrighteous. If you love only those who love you what reward will you get. Are not even the tax collectors doing that? And if you are greeting only your brothers, what are you doing more than others. Do not even pagans do that? Be perfect even as your heavenly Father is perfect."

Banish the concept of enemy from your heart and you will become a powerhouse of God. Your morality must rise far above that of the earthlings and your character must be spotless even as God is perfect.

"Be careful not to do your acts of righteousness before men, to be seen by them. If you do, you will have no reward from your Father in heaven. So when you give alms to the poor, do not blow your own trumpet as the hypocrites do in the synagogues and on the street to be honoured by men. I tell you the truth they have received their reward in full. But when you give to the needy, do not let your left hand know what your right hand is doing, so that your giving may be in secret. Then your Father who sees what is done in secret will reward you."

All religions consider helping the less privileged ones to a life of human dignity as the core of righteousness. Righteousness that is godly has godly reward but righteousness that is exhibitionist has exhibitionist reward.

"And when you pray, do not be like the hypocrites, for they love to pray standing in the synagogues and on the street corners to be seen by men. I tell you the truth, they have received their reward in full. But when you pray, go into your room, close the door and pray to your Father who is unseen. Then your Father who sees in secret will reward you. And when you pray, do not keep babbling like pagans, for they think they will be heard because of their many words. Do not be like them, for your Father knows what you need even before you ask."

Prayer is a secret communion with God and answered prayer is the gift of the Father to his children when they live according to the kingdom principle.

This then is how you should pray:
Our Father in heaven,
hallowed be your name,
your kingdom come,
your will be done
on earth as it is in heaven.

Prayer is the privilege of children who have a relationship with the Father, a loving and reverential relationship. The primary concern of every child of God is that his Father's will be done which is the heart of every answered prayer. God's will for men and women is that they should live a holy life befitting his kingdom. When all the people of the earth lead a holy life, his kingdom has come and his name will be hallowed. Conversely, when even God's children live unholy lives, his name is profaned.

Give us today our daily bread.

Forgive us our debts as we forgive our debtors.

And lead us not into temptation,

but deliver us from the evil one.

Man needs bread — spiritual, intellectual and physical. He also needs the forgiveness of God and man for his transgressions: for his lack of reverence for God and lack of compassion for his brothers. Forgiveness is a full circuit that allows divine energy to flow but unforgiving hearts miss the melody of life and endanger their health. To abandon the path of unrighteousness, one needs God's grace, lest one should get trapped into sin by the evil one.

"If you forgive men their transgressions, your heavenly Father will also forgive you. But if you do not forgive men their transgressions, neither will your heavenly Father forgive you." Forgiving is a means of receiving forgiveness, without which no human soul can stand before the Righteous God.

"When you fast, do not look somber like the hypocrites do, for they disfigure their faces to show men they are fasting. I tell you the truth, they have received their reward in full, But when you fast, put oil on your forehead and wash your face, so that it will not be obvious to men that you are fasting, but only to your Father who is unseen; and your Father who sees in secret will reward you."

The truly religious and the hypocrite both fast; while false fasting gets people's recognition, true fasting gets God's reward.

"Do not store up for yourself treasures on earth, where moth and rust destroy, and where thieves break in and steal. But store up for yourself treasures in Heaven, where moth and rust do not destroy, and where thieves do not break in and steal. For where your treasure is, there your heart will be also."

Treasures of this world are dusts of eternity but heavenly treasures glitter beyond time. Wisdom dictates storing up heavenly treasures in place of dust. And what are heavenly treasures but the good deeds men do to their fellow beings.

"No one can serve two masters. Either he will hate the one and love the other, or he will be devoted to the one and despise the other. You cannot serve God and money."

In the life's bazaar, money replaces God because of its purchasing power. Money has time and again proved to be a good servant but a miserly master. Do not shun money because you are a child of God but use it wisely for the extension of the kingdom.

"Do not worry about your life, what you will eat or drink; or about your body, what you will wear. Is not life more important than food, and the body more important than clothes. Look at the birds of the air; they do not sow or reap or store away in barns, and yet your heavenly Father feeds them. Are you not much more valuable than they? Who of you by worrying add a single hour to his life?

"And why do you worry about clothes. See how the lilies of the field grow. They do not labor or spin. Yet I tell you, that not even Solomon in all his splendor was dressed like one of these. If that is how God clothes the grass of the field, which is here today and tomorrow is thrown into the fire, will he not much more clothe you, O you of little faith... But seek first his kingdom and righteousness, and all these things will be added to you as well."

Worry stems from lack of trust in God and even the faithful at times succumb to it. The first principle of the kingdom is to seek God who is the sovereign King of the universe and the things you need will be simply provided to you.

"Do not judge, or you too will be judged. For in the same way you judge others, you will be judged, and with the measure you use, it will be measured to you."

When you are hypercritical of others, they too will be hypercritical of you. But a positive and benevolent view of others will promote harmony. In any case, Jesus did not mean a ban on judiciary because the judges judge.

"How can you say to your brother, 'Let me take the speck out of your eyes when you have a beam in your own eye.' You hypocrite, first take the beam from your own eye and then you will see clearly to remove the speck from your brother's eye."

Overzealous to correct others, we fail to examine ourselves. Sanctification is the life-long preoccupation of the children of the kingdom because that is the will of God. They have little inclination for carping criticism, which they leave it to the hypocrite.

"Do not give dogs what is sacred, or cast your pearls before swine, for they trample them under their feet and turn to you and tear you to pieces."

Holiness is befitting the kingdom but dogs and swine outside have no use of it; they may even turn and attack you for offering them what is sacred. Gospel communicators therefore have to be truly discerning.

"Ask and it will be given to you; seek and you will find; knock and the door will be opened."

Ask, seek and knock are the three operative principles of the kingdom; seek God with all your heart and you will find him, knock persistently at Heaven's door and you will commune with God, and ask more of the Spirit of God and you will lead a victorious Christian life.

"Which of you if his son asks for bread will give him a stone. Or if he asks for a fish, will give him a snake. If you then, though you are evil, know how to give good gifts to your children, how much more will your Father in heaven give good gifts to those who ask him;" 'Expect great things from God, attempt great things for God,' said William Carrey the great missionary. The children of the kingdom have every right to expect great things from God.

"Do to others what you would have them do to you, for this sums up the law and the prophets."

You will appreciate people better when you learn to empathise with them. The whole scripture could be condensed into one sentence: Do good to others. And when you practise that, you will find the joy of life that most people miss.

"Do people pick grapes from thorns or figs from thistles. Every good tree bears good fruit, and a bad tree bears a bad fruit. A good tree cannot bear bad fruit, and a bad tree cannot bear good fruit. By their fruit you will recognise them."

Know people by their deeds, not by mere words. The godly cannot work deception nor the hypocrite godly deeds.

"Therefore everyone who hears these words and puts them into practice is like a wise man who built his house on the rock. The rain came down, the stream rose, and the winds blew and beat against that house; yet it did not fall, because it had its foundation on the rock." Internalising the Word imparts the power and wisdom of God, but idle listening comes to naught.

"But everyone who hears these words and does not put into practice is like a foolish man who built his house on sand. The rain came down, the streams rose, and the winds began to beat against the house and it fell with a great crash."

Wise men and fools both build houses with the same material; but wise men wisely choose their foundation while fools manifest their folly. Build your life on the person of Jesus Christ — the Rock of Ages — and your house will stand against the floods and storms of this life.

FAITH HEALS

It is amazing that a Roman centurion came to believe in Jesus Christ. A man of generous disposition, this centurion had built a synagogue and earned the gratitude of the Jews. When his servant became seriously ill, the Jewish elders came to Jesus and pleaded with him to visit the centurion's home and heal the servant. And seeing Jesus afar off, the centurion sent word: "Lord, I am not worthy to receive you at home. Just command and my servant will be healed."

Marvelled at his spiritual insight, Jesus comments: "Greater faith I have not found even in Israel." Instantly the centurion's servant was healed.

Jesus was deeply moved by the sight of the only son of a widow being carried in a coffin to the burial ground, at the town gate of Nain. The wailing and moaning of the mother was heartrending. Jesus ordered the coffin to be stopped. Then the Son of God touched the coffin and the widow's son came back to life. The gospels record three instances where Jesus raises the dead.

You thought God's anointed could never be disillusioned? John the Baptist had been languishing in prison over a year after a brilliant career whose highlights included admonishing King Herod the Tetrarch in his own palace. His infamous marriage to his brother Philip's wife while the latter was still alive set bad moral standards for his kingdom. In prison, John could see only darkness and despair, and he fell into the abyss of his vocation. He begins to doubt whether Jesus was really the Messiah or should

Israel expect someone else because nothing seems to be happening. Delay dampens the spirit of even the prophets who expect life to be a quick succession of drama without a pause.

Jesus ministers to John's flagging spirit by the Word of God, "The blind receive sight, the lame walk, the lepers are cured, the deaf hear, the dead are raised and the good news is preached to the poor." Messianic pictures prophesied by Isaiah some 600 years ago were presented to John as a reminder.

In his finest rhetoric elegance Jesus asks his disciples: "What did you go out into the desert to see? A reed swayed by the wind? If not, what did you go out to see? A man dressed in fine clothes? No, those who wear fine clothes are in king's palaces. Then what did you go out to see? A prophet? Yes, I tell you, and more than a prophet." Schools of rhetoric flourished in ancient Greece and Rome under renowned teachers. Generals and statesmen like Alexander, Caesar and Antony — and much later Napoleon — found it a potential weapon, who swayed the world by their sword and the word.

Watch out for *you* in Jesus' sermons that strike an instant rapport with the audience. In the Sermon on the Mount we have many of *you*. You are unique because there is no other person on earth like you. The Hebraic dualism 'what did you go out to see?.".. `then what did you go out to see?' builds up a logical climax to the exposition.

"Yet he who is least in the kingdom of Heaven is greater than he. I tell you the truth: Among those born of women there has not risen anyone greater than John the Baptist." The contrast between John's nothingness on earth and his greatness in the kingdom compels our attention. The great ones of this world will scarcely find their place in the kingdom and the great ones in the kingdom are unlikely to be so in this world.

John went without eating and drinking and they said he is demon-possessed; Jesus went to eat and drink and they say he is a glutton and a drunkard and a friend of tax collectors and sinners.

"But wisdom is proved right by her actions." He who acts wisely indeed acts godly.

Wisdom leads to truth and truth, turning away from sin. "Woe unto you Korazin, woe unto you Bethsaida, woe unto you Capernaum..." These cities of Galilee saw the works of Jesus, but did not repent of their evil ways because men loved darkness more than light. "And you Capernaum, will you be lifted up to the skies? No, you will go down to the depths. If the miracles that were performed in you had been performed in Sodom, it would have remained to this day." Rejection of truth surely invites divine judgement.

THE PHARISEE'S DINNER

Simon the Pharisee invited Jesus to dine with him not so much for a blessed time as to spot something amiss in his conduct. The Pharisees have keen eyes, sharp tongue and indefatigable energy in finding other people's faults and broadcasting them.

In walked a woman of ill repute, tormented by the guilt of her past. She wept bitterly at Jesus' feet, washed them with her profuse tears and anointed them with a jar of perfume. She knew Jesus could give her a New Life and a break with her sinful past.

That was the moment of truth for Simon who laughed within pretty certain he had Jesus in his trap. Simon thought: 'If he were a prophet he would have known what kind of woman touched him.'

Jesus divined Simon's thought and said, "Simon, I have something to tell you. Two men owed money to a moneylender. One owed him five hundred denarii, and the other fifty. Neither of them had the money to pay back, so he cancelled their debts. Now which of them will love him more?"

"The one who had greater debts," answered Simon without realising he was one of the characters in the story. "Do you see this woman? I came into your house. You did not give me water for my feet, but she wet my feet with her tears and wiped them with her hair. You did not give me a kiss, but this woman, from the time I entered, has not stopped kissing my feet. You did not pour oil on my head, but she has poured perfume on my feet.

Therefore, I tell you, her many sins have been forgiven – for she loved much. But he who has been forgiven little loves little." Simon and his other guests began to wonder, `who is this who even forgive sins?' Jesus said to the woman, "Your faith has saved you, go in peace."

Simon thought he was too good and too righteous to treat Jesus on par and missed the joy of salvation. The woman truly repented, was forgiven, and went home with heavenly joy. No one in the world is too bad for the kingdom if he/she repents.

Jesus had many disciples who supported his ministry among whom were women. St. Luke names Mary Magdalene, often identified as the woman who came to the Pharisee's house, Joanna the wife of Cuza who was manager of Herod's household, and Susanna of whom nothing much is known but possibly one of St. Luke's source for writing the gospel.

Every public speaker will encounter four kinds of listeners among the audience: the wayside listener, the rocky listener, the thorny listener and the responsive listener. The wayside listener is drawn by curiosity rather than commitment; the rocky listener listens by sheer inertia and listens with one ear and let go through the other; the thorny listener may reproduce every word of the speech but he is preoccupied with the thorns and thistles of this world; only the responsive listener responds to turn words into actions.

Jesus told a parable to expound the Word in the heart of man. A farmer went out to sow his seed. As he sowed, some fell by the wayside, and was trampled, and birds devoured it. Some fell on rock and sprang up but withered because it lacked moisture. And some fell among thorns but sprang up only to be choked. But others fell on good ground and sprang up, yielding a crop of a hundred fold. The seed is the Word of God and the soil, the condition of the heart. The wayside is the stony heart where the Word cannot dwell; the rocky soil is the fickle heart where nothing lasts; the thorny soil is the sensuous heart where hedonism prevails; and the good earth is the receptive heart that yields a bumper harvest.

The children of God ought to be creative listeners to influence society.

Parables are mini short stories describing familiar objects or situations with a startling moral. By linking the known to the hidden, parables point to a spiritual truth. Parables force the listeners to think and discover for themselves the truth. They conceal the truth from the enemies of the kingdom who are spiritually blind and reveal the depth of meaning to the spiritually discerning. However, care must be taken not to over-interpret parables, each of which is built around a central message.

Then came his mother and brothers seeking to meet him but could not because of the crowd. Engrossed in his Father's business, private moments are a luxury for Jesus. "Mother and brothers are those who hear God's Word and put it into practice," he told his audience — not to belittle his mother or brothers but to remind the audience that they truly belong to the family of God.

The Sea of Galilee could be treacherous deceptively calm one moment and bursting into a squall the next moment. As fishermen the disciples knew it only too well and this time it was just as they feared. Caught in the storm in the middle of the lake, the boat began to rock and it was at the point of sinking when the waves billowed over into it. The disciples loathed waking up their Master but they could wait no longer: "Rabbie, don't you care, we drown," they cried. "Be still," commanded Jesus and at once the storm ceased and the sea became calm. Turning to the disciples he asked: "Where is your faith?" But they were too terrified to reply and overawed by his power over nature.

A creature in human form with no shred of civilization! That hideous-looking man was the perfect figure of a lunatic, so violent that he broke his chains and no one could go near him. He ran menacingly towards Jesus and his disciples as they reached the other side of the lake, stared at the Lord and screamed, "Jesus, Son of the Most High God, do not torment me, or send me to the abyss, I pray."

Jesus commanded the evil spirit to come out of the man. That very moment there was a commotion among a herd of pigs that became violent, ran helter-skelter and jumped headlong into the lake and drowned. Soon there was a bigger commotion when people gathered in large numbers to witness what had happened. The insane was sitting at the feet of the Master, dressed and quiet like a lamb. They were upset that their pigs died and asked Jesus to leave their town — the town that prized the pigs more than the gospel! The insane who was healed wanted to follow Jesus, but he was told to stay back as a witness to God's work in that town.

Across the lake, a crowd was waiting for Jesus. Among them was Jairus, a ruler of the synagogue, whose only daughter was at the point of death. Jesus went home with him, followed by a milling crowd when he suddenly stopped to ask, "Who touched me?" Almost everyone did, who walked before, beside and after him. The disciples found it absurd, because the crowd was constantly pressing on him. Yet he insisted, "Some one touched me. I know that virtue has gone out from me."

Trembling with fear came forward a woman, who touched the tip of his garment and was instantly healed; she was bleeding for 12 years and had spent a fortune on doctors. The touch of faith seldom fails to move the heart of the divine. According to the Jewish custom, if a menstruating woman touches a man he becomes unholy; and no rabbi will talk to a woman in public, let alone touch or teach her. Society considered women second-rate citizens but not Jesus.

Meanwhile word came from Jairus' home that his daughter was dead. "Don't be afraid; believe and she will be healed," Jesus assured him. At Jairus' home, Jesus told the mourners the lass was only sleeping, but they laughed him to scorn. He drove out of the room every one except her father and mother, and his three disciples Peter, John and James. Jesus looked to Heaven, talked to his Father and said, "My child, get up." Her spirit returned and at once she got up.

DECEIVER OR MESSIAH?

Even his own brothers were sceptical of his claim and demanded that he should go to Jerusalem and reveal himself to the nation. There was an element of sarcasm hidden in their words because the Jewish leaders were plotting to kill him. Ever on his Father's schedule Jesus replied, "My time has not yet come."

Amidst the feast of Tabernacle, Jesus made a dramatic appearance in Jerusalem. People were indeed looking for him; some said he is a good man, some said he is a prophet, others said he is the Messiah; yet others said he is a deceiver. Aristocrats who kept an opulent life-style imitating their Roman masters maintained a dignified silence, because the comforts they enjoyed was more important to them than the truth of God; and those who held positions in society merely articulated the views of their religious rulers for fear of excommunication. And those who have nothing to lose galvanised around the prophet of Nazareth, their hope in life.

His boldness astounded the audience and he spoke with authority unlike the rabbis who frequently quoted dead rabbis to establish their authority.

"My teaching is not my own but it comes from my Father. You do not know him yet. But I come from my Father, and I am here only for a short while; and I will go back to my Father... If anyone is thirsty, let him come to me and drink. Whoever believes in me, streams of living water will flow from within him."

Symbolic words convey deeper spiritual truths — difficult for worldlings to grasp. The Living Water is a metaphor for the Spirit of God dwelling in a person when he trusts the Son of God. The Spirit guides the new believer to greater knowledge of God and imparts deeper joy in his heart, which he would like to share with others. That is the only reason why he witnesses God even in the face of persecution.

"Can the Messiah come from Galilee?" some asked. The nervous High Priests and Pharisees sent their temple guards to arrest him. They listened to him with rapt attention and came back overwhelmed: "Man never spoke like him."

"The mob who does not know the law are cursed," promptly proclaimed the Pharisees.

"But does our law condemn anyone before hearing him?" asked Nicodemus to their chagrin.

"Are you also from Galilee, Nicodemus?"

They brought before Jesus a woman caught in the act of adultery laying a trap for him. Should he say "let her go free" as the law of compassion demands he has already set aside the law of Moses. And should he say "stone her to death" as the law of Moses demands then they could ask him to cast the first stone and he would instantly lose his popularity. More over he could be charged with murder under the Roman dispensation. In either case his prophetic ministry will be in peril, they thought.

Jesus challenged the Pharisees to prove their holiness before accusing the woman whom they cleverly trapped. "If anyone of you is without sin, let him cast the first stone," he said. And he stooped and wrote with his finger, according to one commentator, the names of her accusers and the exact time they committed adultery and one by one they left the scene. Jesus and the woman were left alone.

"Where are your accusers? Do no one accuse you?" he asked. "No Sir," she replied.

"Neither do I accuse you," Jesus said and added, "Woman, sin no more."

Forgiveness is the unique aspect of Christ's teaching.

Teaching in the temple, Jesus said, "I am the Light of the world. Whoever follows me never walks in darkness, but have the light of life." Jesus was speaking from the court of women where the offerings were put and where candles burned to symbolise the pillar of fire that led the people of Israel through the wilderness. The pillar of fire represented God's presence, protection and guidance.

The Pharisees challenged him, "You are your own witness, hence your testimony is not valid." According to the Jewish law, you need the witness of two or three to prove a point.

"My testimony is true because I know where I come from and where I am going. Besides me, my witness is my Father who sent me." Three of the greatest questions in the realm of philosophy are: Where do we come from, where are we going and what are we doing here. Anyone who knows the answers merits our attention.

"Where is your Father?"

"You neither know me nor my Father. I go where you cannot come, and you will die in your sins if you don't believe that I came from the Father."

The faces of the Pharisees were burning with rage, unable to comprehend him, unable to engage him in a debate, and unable to command the situation. The point Jesus wanted to make is how little they knew God. Since they have closed their eyes to Jesus they have closed their opportunity to know God and his plan of salvation for them. The dire consequence is they will perish in their sins. This superb artist communicates in the optimum economy of words.

"When the Son of Man is lifted up, you will know who he is. I don't speak anything on my own but what the Father has taught me. I always do what is pleasing to my Father." Jesus speaks and does what delights the Father most because he is the perfect Son of the perfect Father.

"If you keep my teaching, you are my disciples. Then you will know the truth and the truth shall set you free." Jesus himself is the truth and the perfect standard of righteousness. He frees us from self-deception and from deception by Satan, which is called sin. This newfound freedom helps us love and serve God better.

"We are Abraham's children, never a slave to anyone."

Sin has a way of enslaving, dominating, and dictating. "Everyone who sins (violates God's moral law) is a slave to sin. A slave has no place in the family but the Son has. So if the Son sets you free, you will be free indeed. If you were Abraham's children, you would do what Abraham did - believe. Since you tried to kill me, you are the children of your father, the devil. He was a murderer from the beginning and has no truth in him. When he speaks lies, he speaks from his own." Habitual liars are as much the children of the devil as people who disbelieve God. Disbelief, lying, jealousy and murder all are retrograde steps to human disaster.

"You are demon-possessed."

Juxtapose the exalted exposition of Jesus and the petty fogging of the Pharisees. Character assassination is the devil's favourite past time and the devil's children revel in it.

"I am not demon-possessed. But I tell you the truth, if anyone keeps my word he will never taste death."

Slander and vilification never stops a man of God — let alone the Son of God — from doing what is right. Jesus now introduces the concept of eternal life, of which the Jews had only a vague idea.

"Abraham died, so did the prophets. How then did you say if anyone keeps your word he will never die? Are you greater than Abraham?"

Closed minds seldom grasp the truth.

"Your father Abraham rejoiced at the thought of seeing my day, he saw it and was glad."

Jesus puts Abraham in perspective to their annoyance.

"You are not yet 50, then how did you see Abraham?"

"Before Abraham was, I am."

Jesus was logically building up the exposition to this flash point. One needs a bit of Old Testament background to understand the import of Jesus' statement. At the Burning Bush where God reveals himself to Moses, He says, 'I am that I am.' Which means `I am the sovereign, the unquestionable One, the Original cause.' Jesus is saying precisely that, `I am that I am.'

The Jewish leaders need no more provocation and took stones to stone him.

Incredible claims on the first hearing, beginning with 'I am the Light of the world' implying he illumines lives, and 'I know where I am coming from and where I am going' implying omniscience, and 'If the Son sets you free you are free indeed' implying the power to forgive sins, and 'If you keep my word, you will never taste death' that is spiritual separation from God implying the power to grant eternal life, and finally 'I am' ('that I am'), which is the Jewish title for God implying equality with Him.

No wonder the Jewish leaders acted the way they did. Jesus did what they could not — healed and worked miracles that drew large crowds. His words and works challenged their perception of religion and God. The five claims that Jesus makes centres on his divinity and equality with God, which they could not refute. Barbarians respond barbarously, which they did. Stone for truth!

Jesus slipped out of their presence, unscathed, unharmed, the way he slipped out of the hostile synagogue at Nazareth.

THE GOOD SAMARITAN

Of all the parables of Jesus the most dramatic one that caught on universal imagination is the Good Samaritan. In an ironic enactment of the Sermon on the Mount the untouchable Samaritan teaches the Jew the meaning of humanity. St. John's first epistle is built on this theme: he who loves his brother has already kept all the commandments of God.

The parable is an answer to a lawyer's question, "Who is my neighbour?" To put it in context, this lawyer comes to Jesus with, perhaps, the most meaningful question ever asked, ``What shall I do to inherit eternal life?''

"What is written in the law?" asked Jesus in reply.

"Love the Lord your God with all your heart and with all your soul and with all your strength and with all your mind, and love your neighbour as yourself." The lawyer was well acquainted with the Book of Deuteronomy which every Scribe and Pharisee knew almost by heart. Wanting to be commended, the lawyer asked, "Who is my neighbour?" Thus unfolds the parable:

A man was going down Jerusalem to Jericho and he fell into the hands of robbers who stripped him, beat him and left him half-dead.

A Priest came that way, saw the man and passed by the other side. So did a Levite who came that way. Then came a Samaritan who had compassion on him, bandaged his wounds pouring oil and wine, took him on his own donkey to an inn and attended on him. The next morning he took out two silver coins, gave them to the innkeeper and said, "Look after him well. If you spend anything more, I will pay when I come back."

"Which of the three, do you think, was a neighbour to the man who was robbed?" Jesus asked.

"The Samaritan," replied the lawyer.

"Go and do likewise."

The parable has all the elements of a drama – lively characterisation, a powerful theme, a gripping plot and a storyline. The portrayal is pictorial and the setting all too familiar for his audience who might have travelled down that perilous road many a time and each time with the fear of being robbed. Anxiety and tension is built to a suspenseful climax – the right setting for the Good Samaritan deed. Ironically, the priest and the Levite who ought to teach that the heart of godliness is compassion are the ones who need to be taught.

Obsessed with specious holiness, the priest was afraid to touch the half-dead man who could die any moment making him instantly unholy. The Jewish law declares that anyone who touches the dead remains unholy for seven days. Ever since his creation, the Good Samaritan has never stopped indicting the hollowness of the holy order.

Now contrast the three philosophies – those of the robber, the Priest and the Good Samaritan. 'Yours is mine' is the robber's philosophy and 'Yours is yours and mine is mine' is the Priest's philosophy while 'Mine is yours' is the Good Samaritan's philosophy. The theologies behind these philosophies and the gods these men worship — the god of Existentialism, the god of Ceremonies and the god of Compassion — truly intrigue the listeners. The Mafia, Sophia, and Gloria the theologians speak of neatly fit into the parable.

There was a dear little home in Bethany, near Jerusalem, that Jesus was fond of. Two sisters, Martha and Mary, and their brother

Lazarus stayed there. Martha, presumably the elder one, was busy preparing meal for Christ and his disciples while Mary sat at the feet of Jesus and listened to every word he was preaching. Fretting and fuming came Martha to complain to Jesus about her sister's un-sisterly attitude, "Lord, don't you care that my sister has left me to do the work by myself? Tell her to help me!"

"Martha, Martha, you are worried and upset about many things, but only one thing is needed. Mary has chosen what is better, and it will not be taken away from her." The Word of God expounded by the Son of God should take precedence over everything else — even playing the good host.

Through a cluster of eight parables Jesus conveys a message that should shellshock the materialistic apes who think spiritual things do not matter. One rich farmer had a bumper crop such as he had never seen all his life, and his granary would not contain it. "I will build a super-granary; and I will say to myself, 'Eat, drink and make merry the rest of your life,' " he mused. Should the man die that very night he dies a rich fool never having known the living God and having to stand before the Judgement Seat which even the escapist cannot escape.

A man planted a fig tree in his vineyard and every year he looked for fruit but could not find any. After three years of great expectations the owner told the vineyard keeper, "Cut it down, why should it waste soil?" The vineyard keeper said, "Sir, leave it alone for one more year; and I will dig it around and fertilise it; if it bears fruit next year, fine; otherwise, cut it down." Jesus had been ministering to Israel for three years, yet it bore no fruit. Implied in the parable is Jesus asking his Father to spare Israel for one more year and if the nation does not respond let judgement visit it.

A farmer finds weeds growing along with wheat plants but tells his servants not to pluck them before harvest because by chance some of the wheat plants might get uprooted. So he waits for the day of harvest when the two are clearly discernible by the fruit and orders his servants to bundle the weeds and throw them into the fire and then gather the wheat to his barn. The good and the wicked cohabit the earth but clearly they will be sifted and the wicked consumed in the wrath of a righteous God.

Good heavens! A man stumbled upon a hidden treasure in a field. He hurriedly came back home, sold everything he had and bought that field. A merchant looking for priceless pearls suddenly came across the rarest of rare pearls. He, too, hurriedly went back home, sold everything he had and bought that pearl. These two displayed remarkable diligence in acquiring the priceless treasure and were willing to pay any price. The kingdom of God is the hidden treasure and the rarest of rare pearl that no price is too great to possess it.

A man planted the mustard seed in his field. From the smallest of seeds it sprouted to be the biggest of plants sheltering the fowls of the air. So spectacular is the growth of the kingdom. A woman mixed a little yeast with a large amount of flour and soon the yeast permeated through the entire dough. A few godly men can transform a large lump of people in society.

A net caught all kinds of fish in a lake – the tasty ones and the tasteless ones. Brought to the shore the fishermen sorted out the good ones and burnt the bad ones in an oven. So will be at the end of Ages when the wicked of the earth will be cast into the Lake of Fire.

These eight parables blend to give a powerful warning to the spiritually reckless. The first three are parables of Folly – the folly of the rich farmer, the folly of Israel and the folly of the wicked. The next two are the Priceless parables proclaiming the worth of the kingdom is beyond human reckoning. And the next two are the Impact parables demonstrating the impact of the kingdom. The last is the Alarm Bell parable that if you have not woken up by the seven parables the time to wake up to the spiritual truth is now. One of the major themes of the Bible is God's Last Judgement. In spite of the eight-fold warning if you miss the point, you only have to blame yourselves. You probably thought truth is fiction!

Book Four

THE BREAD OF LIFE

Why do people travel miles and miles to listen to a famous orator, or see a great theatrical performance or listen to a world-class musical concert? Whenever Michelangelo's sculptures and paintings were exhibited in Florence and Rome, people went wild with excitement. Leonardo's paintings drew art lovers across Europe to the Eternal City — especially the Last Supper. When Beethoven's 'Seventh Symphony' was played in Vienna, the crowd went on clapping for full 15 minutes after the concert and still would not stop that the police officer on duty had to order the people to vacate the auditorium. Indeed art rules the heart and sends ripples and waves that people cannot resist.

Jesus Christ drew large crowds even in the desert because his sermons touched their lives. It was a time of unprecedented hardship. To maintain its opulence and luxury, Rome levied taxes on her vassal states, which became a burden for the poor and middle-class, because the rich always knew how to milk the system. The economic hardship led to social and political tensions, the cumulative effect of which could be seen in many people becoming mental wrecks or 'demon possessed' as they were commonly thought of. The people were looking for a Redeemer who would liberate them from this hardship and bondage. What made the Jewish religious leaders nervous about the rising popularity of Jesus was that he could be a potential threat to their business interests and even their seat of power because Rome could install him in their place when the people make repeated representations.

Once in a desert place near Capernaum where he went to be alone on hearing the death of John the Baptist, large crowds sought after him. He taught them for three days and healed the sick. When the twilight came, his disciples reminded him the multitude need to go and buy food. Having compassion on the multitude and to challenge the faith of his disciples, Jesus said, "You give them food to eat."

Philip the pragmatic manager said, "200 dinari is not enough to give just one piece of bread to each one of them." Thinking in pure monetary terms, 200 dinari is a man's average wage for 200 days, which is peanuts for feeding the crowd.

Andrew has a different approach. He finds a boy in the crowd, who is willing to forsake his five loaves of bread and two fish and place them into Jesus' hands. All that Jesus needs is a sacrificing heart to turn a crisis into an opportunity. He asks the disciples to make the crowd sit in a row of 50, a mammoth crowd of 5,000, excluding women and children! No one asked why they are sitting in the desert like this; and there was perfect order notwithstanding the great number.

Looking to Heaven, Jesus blesses the bread and fish and gives them to the disciples to serve, and the crowd eat and are satisfied, leaving behind 12 basketful of bread; should we say one each for the unbelieving disciples.

Someone in the crowd had a brilliant idea: make him King so that they don't have to work for bread. The idea found instant acceptance and the crowd was about to forcibly make him King. Knowing their thoughts, Jesus escaped from their midst to a nearby mountain to pray, sending his disciples across the lake by boat. Strong wind was beating upon the boat as the disciples inched their way to Capernaum. It was the fourth watch of the night and still they had traversed just three miles from the shore when they saw a human phantom walking over the sea just 100 yards away. Frightened out of their wits in that stormy scary night they shrieked out and to their great disbelief they heard a familiar voice: "Be of good cheer, it's I".

Peter could not resist the desire to imitate the Lord every possible way and he said, "Lord, if it is you, command me to come to you on water." "Come," said the Lord. And to his great delight Peter started walking on the water and moved close to his Master. But the treacherous wind blew off his courage and to his dismay Simon found himself sinking and he cried out the shortest prayer in the Bible, "Lord, save me." Jesus restores him, rebukes him for his little faith and boards the boat. When the next moment the disciples found themselves on the other side of the lake at Bethsaida near Capernaum, they fell down and worshipped him.

The people on the other side of the lake woke up the next morning to find that Jesus had already left the shore. Soon they ferried across to Capernaum in search of him and finally found him. "You seek me because you ate the loaves and are filled. Labour for the food that leads to eternal life, which the Son of Man will give you," he told the crowd that wanted to make him King.

"What shall we do that we may work the works of God?"

"This is the work of God that you believe in him whom He sent."

"What sign (miracle) will you perform then that we may see it and believe you? Our fathers ate manna in the desert; `He gave them bread from Heaven to eat' as is written."

Clearly, it is not a God-seeking crowd but a circus-seeking crowd desirous of sensational wonders. To win popularity and to rule without coercion, the Roman emperors provided the crowds with bread and circus; and this Jewish crowd demanded the same as a price for their loyalty. Jesus first corrects their scriptural ignorance, "It is not Moses who gave the bread from Heaven but my Father. My Father gives you the bread from Heaven. It is he who comes down from Heaven and gives (eternal) life to the world."

When the crowd that ate the perishable bread across the lake asks for this bread for now and evermore, the stage is set for one of the famous expositions. Pause for a moment to consider how

Jesus turns the desire of the heart into spiritual symbols: to the woman at the well, Jesus speaks of the living water; to the crowd that sought free bread, he speaks of the bread of life; to Nicodemus the seeker after truth, he speaks of being born again; to the furious Jewish leaders who seek to stone him, he speaks of eternal life.

"I am the Bread of life. He who comes to me shall never hunger, and he who believes in me shall never thirst." Jesus speaks of the richness of spiritual life, nourished by the Word in a mysterious way that the world can never understand.

"All that the Father gives me will come to me, and the one who comes to me I will by no means cast out." Those who earnestly seek God — with all their heart, with all their mind and with all their strength — will find Him. It is downright folly not to seek God because the whole purpose of life is to know and glorify Him. And no believer is insignificant in His eyes and His comforting presence is open to the needy all the time.

"I came down not to do my own will, but the will of Him who sent me. This is the will of my Father that I should lose nothing (no one) but should raise them at the last day. And this is the will of Him who sent me that everyone who sees the Son and believes in Him may have eternal life; and I will raise him up at the last day."

In no uncertain terms, Jesus explains why he came into this world: to give the power of resurrection to every life, which is the abiding presence of God in the believer in this life and the life to come. Death has no power to snatch away this abiding presence. And this is the will of the Father.

God's plan for your life is your sanctification, which sharpens your vision and multiplies your efficiency: the sanctified mind receives stimuli from above which people call creativity.

Eternal life is the very life of God in you; while physical death is the separation of your body from the spirit and mind, spiritual death is your separation from the life of God eternally, which is called hell. When a person dies, his body decomposes, and the atoms of his body are scattered in the rivers, in the ocean, in the clouds, back to earth, in a cycle. At the Second Coming, these atoms are miraculously reunited in resurrection. The righteous are resurrected to a life with God which is Heaven and the wicked to a godless life which is hell.

The Jews had problem believing he came down from Heaven. "What says he? His parents, his (cousin) brothers and (cousin) sisters we know. How then he says I am the bread that came down from heaven?"

Now Jesus goes a step further, "I am the living Bread which came from Heaven. If anyone eats of this bread, he will live for ever; and the bread that I shall give is my flesh, which I shall give for the life of the world."

The Jewish listeners were confounded when the imagery shifted from bread to flesh, and when they took him literally. They were baffled when Jesus took the exposition to the climax.

"Truly, truly, I say to you, unless you eat the flesh of the Son of Man and drink his blood, you have no life in you. Whoever eats my flesh and drinks my blood has eternal life, and I will raise him up at the last day. For my flesh is food indeed and my blood is drink indeed."

Today, the mature Christian listeners have no difficulty in understanding the concept of the Holy Eucharist through bread and wine symbolising the flesh and blood of Jesus Christ and the spiritual unity of the believer with the life of Lord.

His flesh and blood is the person and works of Jesus Christ imparting divine life and eternally enriching you. And when Christ lives in you, you have eternal life and you have passed from the realm of death to the realm of life.

"He who eats My flesh and drinks My blood abides in Me, and I in him. As the living Father sent me, and I live because of the Father, so he who feeds on Me will live because of Me. This is the bread that came down from Heaven — not as your fathers ate manna and are dead. He who eats this bread will live forever."

By faith, Christ lives in you and you in Christ. You will know the truth when you begin to experience the reality and richness of the New Life it begets. Christ lives in the Father even as the Father is the fountain of all life; and Christ is the fountain of your life. The fullness of life you will find in God and in God alone.

"This is hard saying, who can listen to this?" said the crowd that wanted to make him King. "It is the Spirit who gives life; the flesh profits nothing. The words that I speak to you are spirit, and they are life." Jesus is telling his audience that they should look much deeper for his meaning because he is speaking of spiritual matters leading to life eternal.

The crowds vanish leaving Jesus and his 12 disciples. And he turns to them and asks, "Do you also want to go away?" Peter has answers for all seasons. "Lord to whom shall we go? You have the words of eternal life. Also we have come to believe and know that you are the Christ, the Son of the living God."

At least one man who stood with that crowd understood even in his own limited way who Jesus is. Of course, he is the chief spokesperson of the group of 12 who wants to be with Jesus and learn from him, no matter what the world thinks of them.

Jesus turned to them and said, "Did I not choose you the twelve and one of you is a devil." There was one among them whose heart was far away from the Kingdom of God and who did not relish the things of the spirit. He was keeping the purse of the group, hoping he would be in charge of the treasury when Jesus becomes the King. A perfect hypocrite, his pretensions deceived all except the Lord, whom he would finally betray.

O WOMAN, GREAT IS YOUR FAITH

Dare you eat with unwashed hands? The Scribes and the Pharisees would bathe away their contamination after a visit to the marketplace where they chanced to meet people outside the faith. For them external cleansing mattered more than internal cleansing: laws of cleansing and ceremonial washing governed their life. To their malicious glee, they discovered that the disciples of Jesus were eating without the ceremonial washing of hand. They indict the disciples for breaking the tradition of the elders.

Jesus in turn points out their ungodly living setting aside the law of God with man-made tradition. Every Jew is commanded to honour his father and mother and protect their dignity in old age by providing for them. Tradition liberated them from their filial obligations by merely saying, 'Qurban', which means 'I have given to God what I should have set apart for my parents' keeping'. They neither gave to God nor to their father and mother but robbed both and pretended to be holy. God is not deceived by this mask of holiness.

"Not what goes into the mouth defiles a man; but what comes out of the mouth, this defiles a man." The Pharisees went away displeased because they loved the praise of men more than the truth of God. His disciples remind him how offended they went — they who were held in high esteem by the people.

"They are blind leaders of the blind. And if the blind leads the blind, both will fall into a ditch." How this leadership bereft of godliness led to the sacking of Jerusalem in 70 AD is history.

Peter was intrigued how anything that comes out of the mouth defiles a man. So the Lord, explains, "Out of the heart proceed evil thoughts, murders, adulteries, fornication, thefts, false witness, blasphemies. These are the things that defile a man, but to eat with unwashed hands does not defile a man."

Jesus was travelling towards the cities of Tyre and Sidon when a woman of Canaan came and cried out, "Have mercy on me, O Lord, Son of David! My daughter is severely demon-possessed." The title Son of David denotes the kingship and the messianic office of Jesus.

But Jesus went on with his journey without a word to the woman. "Lord, send her away, for she cries out after us," said the disciples, implying she has become a nuisance.

"I am sent to the lost sheep of Israel."

Undaunted, she came, fell down and worshipped him, imploring, "Lord, help me."

"It is not good to take the children's bread and throw it to the puppies."

"Yes, Lord, even the puppies eat the crumbs which fall from their master's table."

"O woman great is your faith! Let it be to you as you desire." And her daughter was healed that very hour.

Faith touches the heart of God; no believer has ever returned empty handed from Him. Faith is the hand that receives God's blessings. The Roman centurion, whom we saw in a previous chapter, and this Canaanite woman win Jesus' commendation; but we seldom read about anyone from Israel getting the same commendation.

From Tyre and Sidon, Jesus was travelling to Decapolis and on the way he saw a man, deaf and dumb, brought to him. Jesus spoke to him in sign language raising hope and faith in the man. Then the Lord put his fingers in his ear, spat and touched his tongue. Looking up to heaven, Jesus cried, 'Ephphatha,' which means be opened. The man instantly began to speak and hear.

Resting a while on a mountain, he saw multitudes bringing the blind, the lame, the mute and the maimed to be healed. Jesus healed them and taught the people for three days. At the end of his discourse, he told the disciples, "I have compassion on this multitude... I do not want to send them away hungry, lest they faint on the way."

"How many loaves have you?" he asked. "Seven, and a few little fish too," they replied. He commanded the multitude to sit on the ground. Then Jesus took the seven loaves and the fish, gave thanks, broke them and gave to his disciples. They served a crowd of 4000 and took the remaining seven basketsful.

In Galilee, Jesus ended his public ministry with the feeding of the 5000 and his ministry to the gentiles ends with the feeding of the 4000, and his ministry in Jerusalem would end with a meal in the Upper Room. This living bread that came down from Heaven nourishes the frail human frame to experience the power and mystery of godliness.

At Magdala, a group of Pharisees and Sadducees wanted to see a miracle from Heaven, implying the healing and feeding miracles were not sufficient to get their endorsement. They wanted the Son of God to be a magician performing miracles and entertaining them at their beck and call. They get a sharp rebuke for their ungodly insinuation.

"You hypocrites, you know how to forecast weather by looking at the sky. But you don't know how to discern God's plan and times. A wicked and adulterous generation seeking a sign, and no sign will be given except the sign of Prophet Jonah." Prophet Jonah was in the belly of the giant fish for three days and three nights; and so will be Jesus in the belly of the grave for three days and three nights. (A few hours of the night or day is reckoned as one night or day, according to the Jewish custom). Three years ago, at the first cleansing of the temple, Jesus said, "Destroy this temple, and in three days, I will raise it up," signifying his resurrection as the proof of his divinity. Jesus gave them the proof but they will have to wait. He told the disciples in his characteristic figurative language, "Beware of the leaven of the Pharisees and Sadducees," by which he meant their hypocrisy.

The poor disciples took him literally and thought he was reminding them of the bread they had left behind after feeding the multitude. What specimens of human species! You will find them sleeping when they ought to be praying, and you will find them quarrelling when they ought to be taking up the cross. They represented the foibles and follies of human race in toto.

"O, you of little faith, why do you say you have forgotten the bread? Don't you remember the five loaves and the five thousand and the seven loaves and the four thousand?" Then the disciples understood what he meant.

'WHO DO YOU SAY I AM?'

They came to Caesaria Philippi, a district 25 miles north of Galilee, at the foot of Mount Hermon. It was the ideal setting to open their eyes to the true meaning of life. "Who do people say I am?" Jesus asked, as a prelude to the most important question all of us have to answer one day.

"Some say John the Baptist, some Elijah, others Jeremiah or one of the prophets." Many of his contemporaries thought he was a prophet who spoke the word of God. Now Jesus asks the most important question of all, "Who do you say I am?"

Pat replied Peter who detests delay, "You are the Christ, the Son of the living God."

"Blessed are you, Simon Bar-Jonah, for flesh and blood has not revealed this to you, but my Father who is in heaven." The Father is the source of true knowledge and blessed are those who know the truth.

"You are Peter and on this rock I will build my Church, and the gates of hell shall not prevail against it. And I will give you the keys of the kingdom of Heaven, and whatever you bind on earth will be bound in Heaven, and whatever you loose on earth will be loosed in heaven."

We have come a long way from the Sermon on the Mount to the mystery of the Person of Christ. He came to destroy the works of Satan, which is proliferation of evil, and to establish the kingdom of God on earth. The Church he established should proclaim the life, works, death and resurrection of the Lord till his Second

Coming. The Church should be the light of the world, the salt of the earth, and the city set on a hill, shining like a beacon in the dark.

The Church is made up of living stones who confess that Jesus Christ is the Son of God. It is built on no less a foundation than Jesus Christ himself. Metaphorically, Christ is the groom and the Church his bride, who ought to be pure, holy and eternally loyal. The true Church holds the key to the Kingdom of God, to bind or loose the chains of Satan, and to forgive or remit sins. Peter as the leader-designate is empowered to be the Vicar of Christ after his departure.

The disciples were entertaining the hope that their Master would set up a kingdom in Israel in which they would share the power and glory. The time has come for Jesus to tell them plainly what lies ahead — death on the cross and resurrection. The very idea of suffering is anathema to the human mind and the disciples must have recoiled from it. So Peter takes Jesus aside and gives him 'his wise counsel,' "Far be it from you, Lord: this shall not happen to you!"

"Get behind me Satan." Peter who got the best commendation only moments ago now gets the worst rebuke.

Obsession with the things of this world can blind us to God's truth and His purposes. "If anyone desires to come after me, let him deny himself, and take up his cross, and follow me. For whoever desires to save his life will lose it, but whoever loses his life for my sake will find it. What profit is it to a man if he gains the whole world, and loses his own soul? Or what will a man give in exchange for his soul?"

Nobody knows the price of a soul as best as its Maker. Not all the gold and silver and diamonds of the world come anywhere near the price of a soul, for there is a spark of the divine in every soul. No wonder, the Son of God left all his glory of Heaven and took the human form to redeem the inhabitants of earth.

In God's grand design, the cross comes before the crown:

ironically, the cross is the antithesis of everything the world prizes — power, money and fame. The cross is the epitome of the life of Christ — born in a manger of humility to proclaim God's love, healed the sick and broken-hearted, paid the price for redemption with his own life, descended to the world of the dead to herald the good news, and rose to break the power of the grave, and sat on the right hand of the Father interceding for the believers.

Yet the cross is foolishness for the Greek (read the intellectual) and a stumbling block for the Jew (read the zealous without the true knowledge of God). Since faith does not engage the intellect, the intellectual scorns it; and since the zealot knows nothing of God's love, he stays clear of it. Indeed the cross is the power of God unto salvation. Nothing is more foolish than becoming the most successful person on earth and in the process neglect your inner life. He is the world's greatest loser.

TRANSFIGURATION

Peter, James and John stood on the pinnacle of the high mountain where their Master led them; it was a pinnacle of spiritual experience, too, when the face of their Lord shone bright like a beam of light and his clothes glowing radiant. Bewildered as they looked on, two men — one resembling Moses and the other Elijah — appeared on the scene. Transported spiritually, the disciples said, "Lord, it's good to be here. Let us build three tabernacles, one for you, one for Moses and one for Elijah."

It was a foretaste of Heaven on earth, which is known as the mystery of the Church, where the living and the departed worship together. Moses and Elijah were talking to their Master about the suffering and the cross. His forthcoming visit to Jerusalem did not look very promising as they overheard the conversation: the gentiles would mock him, spit on him, scourge him and finally condemn him to death, all very discouraging for the disciples.

Soon a cloud appeared and everything disappeared. There were peels of thunder like the one at his baptism; and the three fell on their faces, sore afraid. A gentle touch from the Lord put them at ease and they climbed down the mountain to join the rest. Jesus told the three not to talk about it till "the Son of Man rose from the dead."

They had just descended the mountain when they saw a crowd awaiting them. A certain man fell down before him and said, "Have pity on my son who is out of his mind. I brought him to your disciples but they could not heal him."

"O, you men who lack faith," Jesus rebuked the disciples and turned to the man. "Bring your son, here," Jesus said and healed him.

The dismayed nine asked him, "Why couldn't we do it?" "Because you have little faith. If you have faith anything is possible," Jesus said. Faith can uproot mountains (of obstacles) and what is seemingly impossible is possible by faith. Faith begins with experiencing God in the inner realm — through prayer, fasting and feeding on the Word. There is a saving faith, which matures into living faith, and finally fructifies into triumphant faith. The hallmark of triumphant faith is a spirit-filled and spirit-led life bearing abundant fruit. The secret of the ministry of Jesus is his constant communion with the Father, and he would pray the whole night in a lonely place and come back at dawn refreshed and recharged for healing and teaching.

With the cross just six months ahead, he would soon say farewell to Galilee, the scene of many a memorable event in his ministry, and enter trans-Jordan where he would retreat from the crowd to impart intense training to his disciples. Jesus has to prepare the disciples to carry on his ministry to the farthest corners of the earth after his ascension to heaven. Now he reminds them of what is in store for him in Jerusalem that makes them sad. The disciples preferred the kingdom to the cross — the kingdom with all its power and glory; the king sitting on the throne and the disciples, one on his right and one on his left, sitting and holding the imperial court. That raised a heated debate: who would sit on his right and left.

There were too many claimants: The most ambitious eyed on both the seats, taking no chances. Andrew would have preferred the alphabetical order but not Thomas; Peter would have preferred age but not John; Philip would have preferred popularity but not Judas; property and education were tossed about as criteria but were instantly rejected as some would be disqualified. Since the issue could not be solved, it lingered on.

THE KINGDOM WITHIN YOU

It was the most embarrassing moment of their life. Their Master called them and enquired what were they making so much noise over. They who ought to set a shining example living by the Sermon on the Mount were quarrelling among themselves in the first place; they who ought to take up the cross in the spirit of self-denial were quarrelling over who is the greatest in the kingdom; and they felt so ashamed of themselves.

"Whoever wishes to be the chief should serve all. In the gentile kingdom the powerful lord it over, but it shall not be so among you," he said. "The Son of Man came not to be ministered unto but to minister and to give his life a ransom."

Value-based leadership is the art of setting example, especially in excellence of service. Jesus took a child, set him in the midst, and said, "Unless you become like children you cannot enter the kingdom." Behold the cherubic innocence and the guileless face of the child, who is the symbol of inner purity and absolute trust.

John saw a man healing in the name of Jesus and he forbade him. The Master replied, "No man can heal in my name and yet speak ill of me; therefore, do not forbid him." There is power in the name appropriated by a holy life. Evidently, Jesus had other disciples besides the twelve.

The world may condemn the least of men, who are precious in the Lord's sight. So he says, "Whoever shall give a cup of water in my name shall not lose his reward. But whoever shall offend one of these little ones who belong to me, it is better that a millstone were hanged around his neck and cast into the sea."

Keeping your body holy is one of the cardinal principles of the kingdom. Administering a shock treatment, the Lord says, "If your right hand causes you to sin, chop it off: it is better that you enter the Kingdom of God without a hand than enter hell with both hands. Likewise, if your right leg causes you to sin chop it off: it is better that you enter the kingdom of God without a leg than enter hell with both legs." Amputation is not the prescription but purity of the mind and disciplining of the body.

On way to Jerusalem, Jesus and his disciples had to pass through Samaria. But some Samaritans objected to it because the Jews treated the Samaritans with contempt. An enraged James and John asked Jesus to bring fire from heaven and consume these Samaritans.

Jesus rebukes them for their spirit of revenge and reminds them, "The Son of Man came to save not to destroy."

Still on their journey, they came across ten lepers standing afar off and crying, "Master, have mercy on us."

"Go and show yourself to the priests," Jesus commanded. Even as they were going they were healed and one of the ten came back, fell at his feet and worshipped Him. Jesus was amazed that out of the ten only one came back to glorify God. "Your faith has made you well," he told the man.

While Jesus was passing by their town, a group of Pharisees came and asked him, "When will the Kingdom of God come?" "The Kingdom of God is within you," he said. It will not come with visible manifestations as some people fancy.

On the Second Coming, he said it will be as lightning: people will be busy buying and selling, farming and building, marrying and giving in marriage, even as in the days of Noe and Lot. "Two men shall be in one bed, one will be taken and the other left; two women shall be grinding together, one will be taken the other left;

two men shall be in the field, one shall be taken the other left. The righteous of the world will be gathered together and the wicked left out of the kingdom."

Jesus and his twelve crossed River Jordan to Judea. While the Master was teaching in one of the synagogues, the Pharisees asked, "Is it lawful for a man to divorce?"

"What did Moses say?" he asked them.

"Moses permitted it on giving a divorce bill."

"It is a concession to your hardness of heart. In the beginning God created male and female of the species, and for this reason man shall leave his father and mother to cleave to his wife: they shall be one flesh. Therefore, what God has joined let no man put asunder."

They were amazed at his reply but Jesus went further, "Whoever shall put away his wife and marry another commits adultery; and if the woman shall put away her husband and marries another commits adultery."

It was a Jewish custom to bring children to be blessed whenever a great rabbi visited them. So the pious Jews brought their children to Jesus but the disciples forbade them because their Master had come after a long journey. "Let these children come to me: the kingdom of God belong to such," said Jesus, never too tired for those who seek him.

There came someone running to him, kneeled down and asked him, "Good Master, what shall I do to inherit eternal life."

"God alone is good; why call me good. You know the commandments: Do not commit adultery, Do not kill, Do not steal, Do not bear false witness, Do not fraud, Honour your father and mother."

"All these I have been observing since my youth."

Jesus beheld him for a moment and loved him. "Go, sell whatever you have and give it to the poor; you will have treasures in heaven; then take up the cross and follow me."

Away he went, his face downcast, because he was so wealthy.

"It is easier for a camel to go through the eye of a needle than for a rich man to enter the kingdom of God," he remarked.

Peter reminds Jesus that he and others have left everything and followed him.

"Truly I say to you every one who leaves his house, brothers or sisters, or father, mother, wife or children or land for my sake and for the sake of the gospel shall receive a hundred-fold now in the world of tribulation and in the world to come eternal life."

On way to Jerusalem, a third time Jesus mentions his crucifixion. Then came the mother of Zebedee children with their sons James and John, and entreated a special favour from Jesus. "Grant that one of the children should sit on your right and the other on your left in your kingdom." Very thoughtful indeed of the mother who, like the disciples, missed the central point. Jesus is going to Jerusalem not to be crowned but to be crucified and the disciples were fighting over something that did not exist in the physical sense.

"Can you drink of the cup that I drink of and of the baptism I am baptised with?"

"Yes," James and John replied, knowing little what his cup and baptism meant.

"You shall indeed do. But to sit on my right hand and on my left hand is not mine to give; it shall be given to whom it is prepared."

The ten were greatly displeased. Jesus reminded his disciples, "In the gentile (secular) world, the superiors lord it over; but among you those who wish to be first must serve. The Son of Man came not to be ministered unto but to minister and give his life a ransom for many."

THE BLIND SEE

Whom do you call blind — the one who sees or the one who does not? What if the blind man sees what people with eyes do not? Would you still call him blind and what will you call them who refuse to see the truth of God? Follow this man whom they call blind begging in the vicinity of the temple of Jerusalem when Jesus and his disciples were passing by.

"Who sinned, this man, or his parents?" The disciples were reflecting the popular belief of the time that all diseases were caused by sin.

"Neither. It is to reveal God's glory," Jesus said pointing to what he is about to do. Nevertheless, Jesus did not mean this man and his parents are holy without blemish.

Then the Lord spat on the ground, made clay and placed it on the man's eyes as a sculptor would do with his creation.

"Go to the Pool of Siloam," he said, and the man went, washed and instantly received sight.

When his neighbours saw him, at first they did not believe he was the same man. But when they realised what happened they reported the matter to the Pharisees who were indignant because it was the Sabbath.

The poor man was grilled and he had to recount the story again and again. In the end they gave the verdict, "This man is not from God, because he does not keep the Sabbath."

"But how can a man open his eyes, if he is not from God," others countered.

Now they turned to the man and asked him, "What do you say about the man who opened your eyes?"

"He is a prophet."

They summoned his parents and asked, "Is this your son born blind?"

"Yes," they replied.

"How then does he see, now?"

Unwilling to enter into a controversy and fearing excommunication, they said, "He is of age, ask him."

They turned to the man again and said, "Give God the glory! We know this man is a sinner."

"Whether he is a sinner or not, I don't know. But I know one thing: I was blind, now I see."

"What did he do to open your eyes?"

"I told you. Do you want to become his disciples?"

Furious, they retorted, "You are his disciple, but we are Moses' disciples. We know God spoke to Moses; as for this fellow, we do not know where is he from."

"That's strange that you do not know where is he from. Since the world began it has been unheard of that anyone opened the eyes of one who was born blind. If this man were not from God, he could do nothing."

"You are born in sin and you are teaching us?" They could not stand his audacity any more and they expelled the man.

An outcast now, he soon meets Jesus, who asks him, "Do you believe in the Son of God?"

"Who is he Lord, that I may believe in him?"

"You have seen him and he is right now talking to you."

The man fell down and worshipped him.

"For judgement I have come into the world, that those who do not see may see, and those who see may be made blind."

"Are we also blind?" asked some of the Pharisees who heard him.

"If you were blind, you had no sin," he answered. Unbelief is sin; unbelief born of willful refusal to see is sin of the worst kind. God's works are irrefutable and it is human responsibility to recognise and respond. The blind man saw and believed, the Pharisees saw but refused to believe, inviting judgement upon them.

THE GOOD SHEPHERD

"Truly, truly, I say to you, he who does not enter the sheep-fold by the door, but climbs up some other way, the same is a thief and a robber." Jesus is speaking to the same crowd, standing at the same place. He implies that the Jewish leaders are in effect thieves and robbers who lead the people away from God.

"But he who enters by the door is the shepherd of the sheep. To him the doorkeeper opens, and the sheep hear his voice; and he calls his own sheep by name and leads them out."

The exposition of Jesus begins with the familiar — the farmer, the traveller, and now the shepherd. However, to catch the right signal, you need to finetune the mental antenna. The door is the security of the believer and the voice of the shepherd, the voice of the Son of God in the heart of the believer. Believers could be robbed, believers could be misguided, and believers could be retracted. Believers could be vulnerable like the sheep, but they have a security and an inner voice speaking to them, protecting from the evil forces.

"And when he brings out his own sheep, he goes before them; and the sheep follow him, for they know his voice." A good captain leads his troops from the front, protecting his own — very much like the good shepherd. Every believer instinctively recognises the inner voice, guiding him in all endeavours.

"Yet they will by no means follow a stranger, but will flee from him, for they do not know the voice of strangers." Children of God keep away from strange gods, but follow only the living God; they are quick to discern.

"Truly, truly, I say to you, I am the Door of the sheep. All whoever came before me are thieves and robbers, but the sheep did not hear them."

Jesus calls himself the door, the security of the believer and access to the Father. Anyone who stands before the door blocking people's entry is a thief and a robber. He is referring to the Pharisees who have threatened to excommunicate those who confess Jesus as Christ — as they did with the blind man who received sight a short while ago.

"I am the Door. If anyone enters by me, he will be saved, and will go in and out and find pasture." The believer finds eternal security and spiritual pastures because he finds the true meaning of life in Jesus Christ.

"The thief does not come except to steal, and to kill, and to destroy. I have come that they may have life, and that they may have it more abundantly." The diabolic design of Satan is to take people away from God, so that they become his subjects in hell. To this end, he invents false gods and demigods who fulfil human caprices. In contrast, Jesus Christ came to give eternal life to all believers.

"I am the Good Shepherd. The good shepherd gives his life for the sheep. But a hireling, he who is not the shepherd, one who does not own the sheep, sees the wolf coming and leaves the sheep and flees; and the wolf catches the sheep and scatters them. The hireling flees because he is a hireling and does not care about the sheep."

Jesus Christ the Good Shepherd has come to lay down his life for believers. But at the first signal of danger, the hireling and the false shepherd flee to save their lives because they do not own the sheep.

"I am the Good Shepherd; and I know my sheep, and am

known by my own. As the Father knows me, even so I know the Father; and I lay down my life for the sheep." The Hebraic dualism reinforces the truth of the statement 'I am the Good Shepherd.'

The Good Shepherd takes risks to the point of death; and the Good Shepherd knows his sheep. Jesus now unfolds a three-fold relationship between him and his own, between Him and his Father, and between his own and the Father. The word 'know' in the biblical context refers to a deep and intimate relationship of a shared life as that of the husband and wife. And a second time he says he will lay down his life for those of his fold and outside.

"And other sheep I have which are not of this fold; them also I must bring, and they will hear my voice; and there will be one flock and one shepherd." Nothing is more absurd than the concept of Christ for Christians. Christ's mission embraces all humanity without discrimination and his mission is to impart a divine spark in you that you may truly belong to the kingdom.

"Therefore My Father loves me, because I lay down my life that I may take it again. No one takes it from me, but I lay it down of myself. I have power to lay it down, and I have power to take it again. This command I have received form my Father." God alone has life in himself and all other lives are sustained by Him. As the Son of God, Christ has power over life and death – the power to lay down his life at will and the power to take it back at will. Christ came to demonstrate that there is life after death and the Father loves him for that.

There was a division among the audience, some said he has a demon and he is mad while others said a demon cannot open the eyes of the blind.

It was cold December, the time of the Feast of Dedication commemorating the liberation of Jerusalem in BC 164 after a successful guerrilla warfare known as the Maccabean revolt against the Syrian Antiochus Epiphanies who desecrated the temple. Jesus approached the Solomon's porch on the eastern side of the temple which is a covered area protecting from the biting chill.

In their hostility, the Jewish leaders zeroed in to extract a statement which could be used against him. "How long do you keep us in doubt? If you are the Christ, tell us plainly."

"I told you and you do not believe. The works that I do in my Father's name, they bear witness of me." If words are not good enough, his works challenge them to believe — they who saw the blind man's eyes opened.

"You do not believe, because you are not my sheep. My sheep hear my voice, and I know them, and they follow me." Jesus tells them their willful disbelief has cost them dearly as they are outside of the kingdom of God.

"And I give them eternal life, and they shall never perish; neither shall anyone snatch them out of my hand." The forces of darkness cannot snatch that life committed to the Son of God; the enemies of the kingdom could kill the body but not snatch the soul (the inner life) which is secure in God's hands.

"My Father, who has given them to me, is greater than all; and no one is able to snatch them out of my Father's hand. I and my Father are one." The security of the believer is doubly assured — secure in the hand of the Son of God, secure in the hand of the Father. Neither Satan nor his demons or the forces of darkness can snatch the soul of a believer who has committed his life to the Lordship of Jesus Christ.

At the last word, 'My Father and I are one' they took stones the third time to kill him.

"Many good works I have shown you from my Father. For which of those works do you stone me?"

"For a good work we do not stone you, but for blasphemy, and because you, being a man, make yourself God."

"Is it not written in your Law `I said you are Gods'?" If He called them gods to whom the Word of God came, do you say of him whom the Father sanctified and sent into the world, You are blaspheming, because I said, I am the Son of God? If I do not do the works of my Father, do not believe me; but if I do, though you do not believe me, believe the works, that you may know and believe that the Father is in me, and I in Him."

In the Old Testament, men who wrote God-inspired word are called gods in the relative sense. If so when the Son of God whom the Father has sent speaks of himself as one with the Father, how can they call it blasphemy? Who is blaspheming, the one who speaks the truth or those who willfully refuse to see the truth? If they have difficulty in believing that Jesus of Nazareth is the Son of God, believe in the works that he does in his Father's name (authority) and thereby come to the truth. Jesus is speaking so patiently to an audience that sought to stone him because if there is just one person around who wants to escape the judgement for rejecting the truth of God, he is directing his message to that one person.

Truth or no truth, the Jewish leaders were bent on liquidating him. Violence and hostility was moving to a climax and Jesus and his disciples moved to trans-Jordan where Jesus would spent the next few months intensely training his disciples for the task ahead after his departure. It was across River Jordan that John the Baptist began his public ministry and it was here that Jesus would end his public ministry.

DEADMAN LAZARUS

Word came to Jesus at trans-Jordan that the one whom he loved was gravely ill. This loved one belonged to a close-knit family of two sisters and a brother whose parents might have been long dead leaving behind the three to fend for themselves. Jesus loved this hospitable home and made it his abode whenever he was in Jerusalem which is a two miles' journey.

Martha seems responsible for running the house while Mary was the Little Darling of the house and Lazarus the sole breadwinner. The two sisters presented a study in contrast as Martha loved action while Mary loved contemplation. Like the surging surface of the ocean and the tranquillity beneath, the two sisters epitomised the two worlds that merged into one family by godly design.

Engrossed in intensely training the twelve, the Master and his disciples were staying in Village Ephraim on the fringe of the desert of trans-Jordan where John the Baptist was preaching before Herod the Tetrarch beheaded him. Jesus' strategy was to spiritually empower the disciples who would in turn create a chain of disciples living by the dynamic kingdom principle.

For reasons better known to the Lord, he did not respond to the news from Bethany for two days. On the third day, he told his disciples that Lazarus was 'sleeping' and he was going to wake him up. Slow to understanding, the disciples said there was no need to go all the way to awaken Lazarus — a sleeping man will wake up by himself anyway.

"Lazarus is dead," he told them plainly.

In his pessimistic streak, Thomas said, "Let us go and die with him." It was no more safe for Jesus and his disciples to travel through Judea with so much of hostility in the air.

News travelled before him that Jesus was nearing Bethany. Martha ran to meet him and as soon as he was within the audible range cried out, "Lord, if you had been here, my brother would not have died."

"Your brother will rise again," Jesus comforted her. She believed that Jesus could deal with a sick man — not a dead man.

Martha thought Jesus was going to give a sermon, and she replied: "I know he will at the last day."

"I am the Resurrection and the Life," Jesus said. "He who believes in me, even if he dies, I will raise him up at the last day. Do you believe this?"

"Yes, Lord, I believe you are the Christ, the Son of God who is to come into the world," Martha said.

"If you believe, you will see the glory of God."

Martha went back home the way she came, running. Bouncing with energy she was one who would rather hector her way through life than face it calmly. In contrast, Mary the introspecting sat at home, contemplating trying to understand the deeper truths of life through the veil of tears.

Martha told her sister that Jesus was calling her, and only then did she step into the scene. She walked out of the house as gently as she could. The good neighbours thought she was going to the grave to weep, and they followed her. Surely Mary must have been the darling of her neighbours, presumably because of her tender age, transparent sincerity and probably good looks. When Martha stomped out of the house, her neighbours hardly noticed her, but when Mary walked out gently, they followed her.

"Lord, if you had been here, my brother would not have died."

Mary too believed in his power over sickness but not over death and grave, which was yet to be manifested. The great difference between Mary and Martha was that Mary speaks after kneeling down and worshipping him. Among all the people conclaved there Mary alone pays the respect that is due to his deity.

Jesus was deeply moved seeing the tears of Mary and those of others. He was so moved that he himself wept.

"Where have you kept him," Jesus asked.

Martha said, "he had been dead for four days and would stink." She thought he was going to pay his last respects to her brother.

"Remove the stone from his grave," commanded Jesus to the people around. They did not panic at the prospect of the stench poisoning the air they breathe. They obeyed his authority.

"Father, I know that you always listen to me. But for the sake of those standing around me, I pray this, that they may know you have sent me." Jesus prayed thus and then said aloud, "Lazarus, come out."

The dead man Lazarus came out in his grave cloths — hand and foot, head and body bound! They stood pale and aghast in disbelief. "Unbound him," Jesus ordered, and they did, and clothed him with his own.

The rational mind has difficulty in reconstructing something it is not exposed to, and anything it cannot reconstruct it rejects — be it heaven, hell, or a man rising from the grave after three days. The mind takes time to adjust to a new reality like the sudden death of a near-relative, and when the outpouring of grief ebbs the mind begins to accept the reality. Genuine faith needs proof to build on and experiences to sustain it.

The onus of proof of raising Lazarus rests on the Resurrection of Jesus Christ himself, which is a fait accompli. If Jesus is the Son of God, he rose again, and so did Lazarus; if not neither Jesus nor

Lazarus came back to life and Christianity is the most humbug of religions. But Christ's Resurrection is among the best attested of events, with more than 500 people at once witnessing the Risen Christ and at least seven other recorded appearances to the disciples. In fact, the raising of Lazarus is a signpost to his own resurrection only days ahead.

On the site where Jesus performed this miracle stand a chapel to commemorate the event and the tomb of Lazarus adjacent to it. One man's life is another man's death: life for Lazarus meant death for Christ. Alarmed by the growing power of Jesus, the Sanedhrin — the Supreme Jewish Authority of the Jews comprising 70 elders — met shortly thereafter and decide that Jesus should be done away with.

TAKE UP YOUR CROSS

It was indeed an occasion for rejoicing but one man was furious — the ruler of the synagogue. "There are six days in a week to get healed. But not on a Sabbath day," he yelled indignantly.

The scene was a sequel to Jesus healing a woman with a hunchback ailing for 18 years. His heart melted at the plight of the woman whom he called forward. "Woman, you are set free from your infirmity," he said and he touched her. Instantly, the woman stood up praising God.

It was the next Sabbath after raising Lazarus, and Jesus was teaching in a synagogue in trans-Jordan when he spotted the woman among the audience.

"You hypocrites, you untie your ox or donkey on the Sabbath day to lead it to drink. Should I not untie this woman who had been in Satan's bondage for 18 years?" Jesus rebuked him to silence.

Illustrating the kingdom, Jesus said, "What shall I compare the kingdom of God? It is like the mustard seed ..." — the tiniest of seeds growing into the tallest of plants sheltering birds of the air. Small beginning, spectacular growth, and most serviceable by nature: that's kingdom at work.

Popular preachers win instant acceptance by easy virtues and slack spirituality. So, someone among the audience asked, "Is there only very few who enter the kingdom of God?" "Indeed, the gate to the kingdom is narrow and many will try but will not be able to enter." Life in the kingdom demands discipline and sacrifice.

The word 'kingdom' might sound archaic to post-modern ears, but for Jesus' audience the word has not lost its sheen: it was the time of building kingdoms and empires. The first known empire in history, that of Alexander, was only 300 years old, and that of Julius Caesar a living memory.

If the word 'kingdom' has a magnetic appeal, the word 'cross' instantly turns the audience away. It is fraught with the danger of rejection. But God's plans need no consent of man. As God's spirit speaks through Prophet Isaiah:

> For My thoughts are not your thoughts,
>
> Nor are your ways My ways, says the Lord.
>
> For as heavens are higher than the earth,
>
> So are My ways higher than your ways,
>
> And my thoughts than your thoughts.
>
> For as rain comes down, and the snow from heaven,
>
> And do not return there,
>
> But water the earth,
>
> And make it bring forth and bud,
>
> That it may give seed to the sower
>
> And bread to the eater,
>
> So shall My word be that goes forth from My mouth;
>
> It shall not return to Me void,
>
> But it shall accomplish what I please,
>
> And it shall prosper in the thing for which I sent it.

The Pharisees have got rid of God from the heart of their religion and installed in his place a set of man-made laws. Fasting, Sabbath and Passover became the icons of their religion. Jesus challenged the system by healing on Sabbath after Sabbath after, of course, asking them, "Is it lawful to heal on the Sabbath?" He did precisely the same that Sabbath, too, when a Pharisee invited him for meal and he found a man suffering from droopsy. They knew he would heal anyway and so kept their peace. He touched the man, healed him and sent him away. Jesus was demonstrating doing God's work is not breaking the Sabbath.

Grabbing seats of honour in a banquet hall has the imminent danger of public disgrace when the host arrives and asks you to vacate the seat for a dignitary. Choose a seat of less honour so that the host will ask you to move up. In the kingdom, too, the self-seekers will be humbled and the truly humble elevated. When you throw a banquet, invite the poor, the crippled, the lame, and the blind

— the kind of people who cannot return your hospitality — and God will reward your hospitality.

A very rich man once prepared a banquet and sent his servants to remind the guests that the feast was ready, but they excused themselves. One said, "I have bought a piece of land, now I want to inspect it." (An obvious lie because people don't buy and then inspect; rather they inspect twice before they buy). The next man said he bought five yoke of oxen and wants to inspect them (Inspection precedes buying, you liar!). Another man said he was newly married and wanted time off with his bride. In fact, a banquet is a good occasion to be seen together rejoicing (marriage is no hindrance to the heavenly feast).

When the rich man found those invited were unworthy he sent his servants and asked them to fill the banquet hall with all and sundry. And he swore in his wrath that none of those invited would ever taste his feast. The very rich man in the parable is the infinitely rich God who has prepared a spiritual banquet for all humanity. Caught in the snares of vanity, the earthlings — beginning with the chosen race — reject God's invitation. But the perils of spiritual negligence are too real to be glossed over.

Crowds do not make disciples but those who stand out of the crowd. When Jesus saw large crowds following him, he said, "If anyone wishes to follow me, let him take up his cross (deny himself)

and follow me." The cross is the symbol of (super human) sacrifice. Only those who are capable of sacrifice could be his disciples.

No man builds a tower without first calculating the cost, lest with an unfinished tower he become the laughing stock of the town. And a king going to war would first find out the strength of the enemy; should he find his army outnumbered, he would rather negotiate peace.

So know the price of discipleship before you seek to be one.

FATHER'S LOVE

A great teacher is one who makes the incomprehensible comprehensible, the unfathomable fathomable and the invisible visible. Through three expository parables — of the Lost Sheep, of the Lost Coin and of the Lost Son — Jesus brings home to the audience the love of the Father for the lost humanity. Jesus' love for the lost is celebrated, and so is his love for the underprivileged and the outcast of society. Like Father like Son, it reflects his divine character, which the self-seeking Jewish leaders hated. They became hyper critical of Jesus, for he preferred the company of tax collectors, harlots, lepers and the blind, the whole unholy lot.

The triad arranged in the ascending order reveals the heart of the Father and his heartache for the lost. A man who owns a hundred sheep — a status symbol in those days — loses one, and he leaves the 99 behind in search of the missing one. And when he finds it, he rejoices more than owning the 99. What is lost and found has a sentimental price attached to it!

A woman who treasures ten silver coins loses one of them. She lights a lamp and sweeps the house till she finds it. And she calls all her friends and rejoices. Even so the Father in Heaven rejoices over his children who have gone astray but have come back.

The most enacted of Jesus' parables is the Lost Son, better known as the Prodigal Son. Three prodigals emerge in the parable, the Father prodigal in his love, the elder son prodigal in his heartlessness and the literally prodigal younger son asking his share of property even while his father was alive — treating his father in effect like a corpse. The prodigal son goes on a long journey, away from home, away from the father, away from God's righteousness and truth, away from the fellowship of saints. Reduced to penury after squandering his inheritance, the prodigal son works for a farmer feeding his pigs and longing for their food, but even that is denied because there is a severe famine in the land.

Good sense returns to him and he thinks of his father's house where even the servants eat to their heart's content. 'If I go back and apologise, perhaps my father will take me back as one of those labourers,' he said to himself, and so severe was the famine that he decides to return. When his father saw him afar off, he ran to meet him, threw his arms around him, hugged him and kissed him. "Father, I have sinned against you and heaven," he said, but did not say, 'take me back as a servant' after seeing his father's prodigal love.

When the elder son came to know his father is preparing a feast for his prodigal brother he was angry — like the Pharisees of his time and the neo-Pharisees of today who delight in branding people. He refused to come home and the father went out to pacify him, "All that I own belong to you." The parable corrects the popular misconception that God is someone to be feared and appeased; and it shows he is our Father who is to be loved, revered and worshipped.

The parable of our time that needs to be preached constantly from every pulpit is the Rich man and Lazarus. A happy-go-lucky man faired sumptuously; dressed up in the best of sartorial elegance and world famous brands; dined and wined in the most expensive culinary delights; and rubbed shoulders with the rich and powerful of his time. He was success personified and a prisoner of the present moment. For him God was a mere joke he could do without. And there lived a beggar in the vicinity whose only friends were spaniels that licked his sores. In contrast, poor Lazarus had nothing to count on and he had all the time for God.

Then came the day of reckoning: both men died and the Rich man was buried in a tomb of pomp and pageantry while angels came and led Lazarus to the company of the righteous departed and Patriarch Abraham. The moment of truth arrived for the Rich man who woke up in hell tormented in the blazing fire. To his utter disbelief he found that 'worthless' beggar Lazarus enjoying the felicities of heaven. In that great theological seminary he learnt in an instant all the profound truths of life — but, alas, hell is truth realised too late. The Rich man now dared not ask whether there is God, whether there is life after death, whether there is a heaven and a hell.

He called Father Abraham and begged him to send Lazarus with a pail of water to quench his thirst because the heat was unbearable. The Rich man to whom one seldom said 'no' was now told there was a big chasm between heaven and hell so that people could not change destinies. He was then burning with a desire to be an evangelist to warn his brothers on earth of what is in store for those who neglect the truth. He had a strong argument to present. If a man rose from the dead and speaks, people will be convinced. "If they don't listen to Moses and the prophets, neither will they listen to someone who rose from the dead," came the reply. Those who are stubbornly blind to the truth will stay blind, even if the Son of God himself will rise from the dead and he is preached every hour in some part of the globe or the other — as is done today.

Eternal truths embedded like jewels in the crown, this parable speaks to the materialistic society.

The vignettes of life and life after death and the startling contrast they present like the Rich man of this world becoming the poor man of eternity and the poor man of this world becoming the Rich man of eternity ought to open the eye of the spiritually indolent.

ZACCHAEUS SEES JESUS

Zacchaeus the Chief Tax Collector is a disturbed man, whom sleep eludes and nightmares haunt. Appetite has long deserted him and his moods are volatile. The root cause: the man has degenerated into a greedy pig!

It is then he hears about Jesus Christ the Physician who heals freely. Zacchaeus longs to see him, and one day while he is walking along the Jeriho-Jerusalem caravan route, he sees a multitude coming across. He is told Jesus of Nazareth is passing by. Unwilling to let go a lifetime opportunity, he climbs a sycamore tree to have a glimpse of the prophet because Zacchaeus is a short man. To his great surprise, the procession halts at the foot of the sycamore tree, and Zacchaeus can neither believe his ears nor his eyes.

"Zacchaeus, come down immediately. I must stay in your house today."

That was Jesus beckoning him. Zacchaeus has a lot of things to set right in his life and he does not hesitate to confess: "Lord, here and now, I give half of my possessions to the poor, and if I have cheated anybody out of anything, I will pay back four times the amount."

Tax collection was extortion in those days since tax collectors could levy four times the prescribed tolls to fatten their coffers with no one to account for except imperial Rome.

In the newfound joy of salvation, Zacchaeus is willing to make restitution and will never barter his joy for some ill-gotten wealth.

As the two walk towards the house of Zacchaeus, some murmur that the Rabbi has gone to sup with a sinner. "The Son of Man came to seek and save that was lost," he tells them. And on reaching Zacchaeus's home, Jesus pronounces, "Today salvation has come to this house ..."

St. Luke excels in spiritual sensitivity by painting touching scenes like the turnaround of Zacchaeus, the conversion of a robber on the cross, and earlier the visit of the shepherds at the manger.

As Jesus was nearing Jerusalem, he told them the Parable of the Talents. A man went to a distant land to become king — that rings a bell with the audience who have not forgotten Herod's journey to Rome to receive the title 'King'. Before setting out, he gave 10 talents each to 10 of his servants to trade and increase the wealth. He was such an unpopular man that his subjects sent him word that they do not want him king over them. Nevertheless, he became king and returned to the land and he called his servants to give an account of what they had done with the talent.

The first servant reported he made 10 more talents with the 10 given him and the king made him ruler over 10 cities. The second gained 5 more talents and the king made him ruler over 5 cities. The third said he buried the talent under the earth because he knew the king is a hard taskmaster who would reap from where he has not sowed. The furious king reprimanded him and ordered that the 10 talents be taken away and given to the first who made 10 more talents. The third servant was self-centred and did not share his master's interests; he is not worthy to be hired because he was disloyal. And the king ordered that all those who opposed him be brought and slaughtered before his eyes. Those who oppose the kingdom of God will not prevail but be dealt with severely. The parable teaches that the time, talent and resources God has given to each one should be multiplied and used for the extension of the kingdom, lest they be taken away.

Simon the Leper prepared a feast for Jesus as a mark of gratitude for healing him. Across Simon's home stayed another grateful family, that of Martha, Mary, and Lazarus whom Jesus raised. As the Master sat for supper, Mary brought a very costly perfume — the cost of which is reckoned as a year's wages in Palestine — and anointed him, and the fragrance filled the whole room.

"Why this waste of money which should have been given to the poor," commented an indignant Judas. Not that he cared for the poor but that he cared for the money, which at times he stole as he was keeping the purse of the group. Mary by her sacrifice and Judas by his coveting reveal their intrinsic worth or worthlessness. For Mary, it was an act of adoration and worship; for Judas, it was an act of sacrilegious since he considers what is spent on the Son of God a waste.

"Do not trouble this woman; she has done it as a memorial for my burial. You have the poor always with you, not me. Wherever the gospel is preached what she did also will be proclaimed." Jesus interprets her deed as symbolic anointing for his burial just two days ahead and thereby immortalises her. In fact, Jesus had a hasty burial without anointing.

Book Five

TRIUMPHAL ENTRY

The embers of Jewish nationalism were aflame during the Passover festival. Excited at the prospect of the Messianic moment, the nation awaited his appearance in the temple. They hoped he would be like Moses the Liberator, like Joshua the Conqueror, like David the Great King. Decimated, vanquished, and exiled, the Jews clung on to the Messianic hope that preserved the nation for two millennia: since 70 AD, they had been nomads dispersed across the globe but this undying hope brought them back to their ancestral homeland after World War II.

An Israeli victory over imperial Rome! Think of Saddam Hussein marching on the Capitol Hill in Washington after the Gulf War! Or Augustus Caesar coming to pay homage to Jesus Christ. Yet in less than four centuries since his triumphal entry to Jerusalem, Rome bowed before Christ. He was crowned King on Palm Sunday and crucified on Good Friday, all in one week. And the kingdom he conquered is the kingdom of hearts — millions of hearts down the centuries.

As he neared Bethphage and Bethany, down the slope of Mount Olives, he sent two of his disciples on a mission. They were to untie a colt on which no man ever rode and bring it to him. Should the owner of the colt ask why, they were to simply say the Master needs it. And at once he would let the colt go.

News spread like wild fire that the Prophet of Nazareth would be in Jerusalem shortly. The crowds, mostly pilgrims from afar off, surged ahead on the famous caravan route that stretched from

Jerusalem to Jericho. Pilgrims from Galilee and Perea turned it into a tumultuous victory procession, so familiar to people living in those empire-building times.

As he mounted the colt, they spread their outer garments on the road as a mark of respect. Some broke branches of trees and spread them on the road; others brought palm leaves symbolic of welcoming kings. When they saw the sea of humanity coming down from Jerusalem to hail the Prophet of Nazareth, they were electrified and shouted spontaneously:

"Hosannah to the Son of David, blessed is he who comes in the name of the Lord, Hosannah in the highest."

That was the coronation of the King of Kings, a humble tribute from frail mortals. It was a spontaneous outburst of pilgrims who heard what happened at Bethany only last week.

Rejoice greatly, O Daughter of Zion!
Shout Daughter of Jerusalem!
See, your King comes to you
Righteous and having Salvation
Gentle and riding on a donkey,
on a colt, the foal of a donkey.

So wrote Prophet Zechariah 400 years before the event seeing it in his vision. They were at Bethphage (the House of Figs), a village at the foot of Mount Olives on the outskirts of Jerusalem, which has lost its identity because of haphazard urbanisation and modernization. Bethphage was the name of a district as well but today it exists only in biblical memory.

They soon lost sight of Bethany (modern El-Azariye) that hamlet perched on a broken rocky plateau on the other side of Olivet. The road ahead is a broad mountain-track, winding over rocks and loose stones. Below and above, you will find fig trees growing out of the rocky soil.

Over the ridge begins the descent of the Mount of Olives

towards Jerusalem and the first view of the city is caught from here. The temple and the northern part of the city are still hid by the slope of the mount on the right, but Mount Sion emerges distinctly. The city rises terrace upon terrace, from the palace of Maccabees to that of the high priest, through castles and towers and magnificent gardens and finally the royal abode of Herod, on the very ground where the palace of David once stood.

As the crowds caught the first glimpse of the city of David, they went hysterical, shouting, "Hosannah to Son of David! Blessed is he who comes in the name of the Lord." The bewildered Pharisees uttered in exasperation, "See, the world is gone after him."

As the road descends, the glimpse of the city is withdrawn behind the ridge. It climbs a rugged ascent and reaches a ledge of smooth rock. And in an instance, the whole city bursts forth into view, with the temple tower dominating the gardens and suburbs.

Just in front, is the Valley of the Kedron seen in its greatest depth joining the Vallley of Hinnom, giving a special effect to the city, as if rising out of a deep abyss.

This is where Jesus wept over the city, wept loud and deep. He could see the Roman legions closing in on the Holy City that rose before him in all its glory and false sense of security. He could see the gory bodies of her children strewn among the ruins of a city that is razed to the ground. He could sense the eerie silence that would descend on the city after death and desolation. Israel to this day knows not the things which belong unto its peace!

The time has come for Jesus to reveal himself as the central person of the scriptures, who will lay down his life and take it back again as foretold by the prophets. Christ's entry to Jerusalem this time was stately – unlike his earlier visits. The time to proclaim his Messiahship is now, the time to proclaim his kingship is now. The time to meet his foes is now, the time to make his supreme sacrifice is now. The time to proclaim victory over death and the power of resurrection is at hand.

But Jesus was not giving himself away to the excitement of the mobs, as some commentators put it. It was on his Father's plan, and everything he did was on His time and in His plan. His reality was his Father's will, every moment of his life.

Jesus taught a new morality and ethics that through him you enter the New Reality. The New Reality of fellowship with the Father and the empowering of the Holy Spirit witnessed through transformed lives. This is the message of Palm Sunday and the mobs who sang Hosannah mostly missed it.

As St. John, in his Book of Revelation, tells us: Before me was a great multitude that no one could count, from every nation, tribe, people and language, standing before the throne and in front of the Lamb. They were wearing white robes and were holding palm branches in their hands. And they cried out in a loud voice:

Salvation belongs to our God,

who sits on the throne,

and to the Lamb.

All the angels were standing around the throne and around the elders and the four living creatures. They fell down on their faces before the throne and worshipped God, saying:

Amen!

Praise and glory

and wisdom and thanks and honour

and power and strength

be to our God for ever and ever

Amen!

What happened at Jerusalem was a pale shadow of the scenes in heaven. As the cries of Hosannah rent the air, a chill went down the spines of the Jewish leaders. The veneration and wild excitement of the multitudes seem to upset all their calculations. Last time when he was in the Temple, they took stones to kill him and he had a narrow escape; but this time he comes with battalions and battalions of crowds that the leaders are impotent with rage. It was no use rebuking them when they were at such frenzied pitch. So they appealed to Jesus whom no doubt they hated but if only to silence the crowds.

"If they keep quiet, the stones will cry out," he said, signifying the heavenly import of the triumphal entry of the King of Kings.

All Jerusalem was taken aback and many asked, 'Who is he?'

They replied, 'This is Jesus, the Prophet of Nazareth of Galilee".

In the Temple, Jesus looked around upon all things. As it was nearing dusk, the pilgrims started departing. Jesus with his twelve went to his second home — the home of Lazarus, Mary and Martha — for some rest before the hectic week begins.

St. Mark clarifies that "Jesus entered Jerusalem and went to the temple, but since it was already late, he went out to Bethany with the twelve." This means Jesus cleansed the temple on Monday; and rested at Bethany on Sunday night, and possibly on Monday, Tuesday and Wednesday nights before his final sacrifice on the cross.

THE SECOND CLEANSING

Monday

Very early Monday morning, Jesus left Bethany with his disciples, presumably for his long prayers at Mount Olives, and then he returned to the temple. On his way to the temple, he was hungry and he saw a fig tree with lush green leaves. Hoping there would be some fruit on it, he walked to the tree; but found none. "May no one ever eat fruit from you again," Jesus cursed the tree.

Alfred Edershemin deals with the theme thus:

> After a nightlong prayer, Jesus felt hungry, and sought food in a fig tree. It is reasonable to assume that the first night of the Passion Week, Jesus spent in solitary prayer. He left Bethany even before dawn with his disciples and on the way to Jerusalem via Mount Olivet, he felt hungry and looked for fruit in a fig tree. It is a well-known fact that in Palestine fruits appear before leaves and even unripe fig once it turns red is eaten by travellers.
>
> Bengel's comment that the manifestation of his true humanity in hunger should be accompanied by that of his divinity in the power of His Word of judgment is apt. The second day of the Passion Week began with the symbolic judgement on the leafy, barren fig tree. The same symbolic judgement will be set forth more clearly in the temple. At the beginning of his public ministry three years ago, Jesus cleansed the temple and now at the end of his public ministry he cleanses the temple once again. If the first cleansing was a teaching and warning, the second was symbolic judgement. What he began in the first, he finished in the second.

It was Passover time then and is now. It was prayer time for the truly religious but profiteering time for Jewish leaders who put up stalls inside the temple. At the first cleansing, Jesus took a cord, made a whip and lashed all those who sold sheep and cattle and exchanged coins inside the Temple; but now he simply drove them out and overturned the tables of moneychangers. Things were pretty bad then, but now they weren't as bad as needing a whip.

Tuesday

On Tuesday morning on their way to the temple, the disciples marvelled that the fig tree that Jesus cursed had withered. Jesus said, "I tell you the truth, if you have faith and do not doubt, not only can you do what was done to the fig tree, but also you can say to this mountain, 'Go throw yourself into the sea,' and it will be done. Therefore, I tell you, whatever you ask for in prayer, believe that you have received it, and it will be yours. And when you stand praying, if you hold anything against anyone, forgive him, so that your Father in heaven may forgive you your sins."

Jesus cursed the fig tree to demonstrate to the disciples the efficacy of prayer life — the epitome of the disciple's effectiveness. Ineffectiveness stems from lack of prayer and lack of faith. Faith is not so much a matter of the lips as that of the heart. Prayer is opening your heart to God and allowing the power and the holiness and the love of God to transform you. Prayer imparts godly character, godly desires, and a godly mind. There is no place for hatred, rancour, malice or jealousy in the heart, for these hinder answered prayers. When a godly person prays, he prays for the things God wants him to pray because he walks with God and knows the mind of God and the will of God in his life. By prayer, he removes the mountain of obstacles that stand in his way. Jesus is not telling his disciples to construct roads and dams and bridges through prayer as some of his critics have construed to misunderstand and misrepresent the imagery of asking the mountain to jump into the sea.

BY WHOSE AUTHORITY?

The chief priests and elders awaited Jesus' entry into the temple courts to challenge his authority. At the peak festive season, he drove away the traders and moneychangers who fattened the chief priests' coffers. Teaching in the temple without their permission violated the cannon and the predators were lying in wait for Jesus to start his sermon so that they can interrupt and show the crowd who runs the temple.

Scarcely had Jesus begun when the authorities swooped and demanded, "By what authority are you doing these things? And who gave you this authority? The Son of God is not accountable to puny little creatures and he shot back, "I will also ask you one question. John's baptism — — where did it come from?"

They discussed among themselves. If they said it was from heaven, he would ask them, 'why then didn't you believe him?' And if they said from men, the crowd will stone them because the people deemed him a prophet, like Isaiah, Jeremiah and Daniel. So they said, "We don't know." To which Jesus said, "Neither will I tell you."

In effect, Jesus is saying 'You don't deserve a reply, but if ever you need one, consider John's baptism which you did not take because you were far removed from God's ways.'

The jewry had the authority but not the power to stop him. He had power over the crowd which they feared and felt powerless. Their impotent rage seething like a volcano would take the conspiratorial outlet to erupt. All it needs is a traitor to facilitate the conspiracy.

Jesus has a genius for inventing parables in a split second to match any situation. "What do you think? There was a man who had two sons. He went to the first and said, `Son, go and work today in the vineyard.'

'I will not,' he said, but later he changed his mind and went. Then the father went to the other son and said the same thing. He answered, 'I will, sir,' but he did not go.

"Which of the two did what his father wanted?"

"The first," they answered without knowing they were condemning themselves.

"I tell you the truth, the tax collectors and the prostitutes are entering the kingdom of God ahead of you. For John came to show you the way of righteousness, and you did not believe him, but the tax collectors and the prostitutes did. And even after you saw this, you did not repent and believe him."

To disbelieve whom God sent is the worst malady of ungodliness. Of the two sons in the parable, the tax collectors and prostitutes represent the son who repented, while the Jewish leaders represent the unrepentant son who professed godliness but did not practise. It is self-deception at its deceptive worst.

If this parable is too subtle, here goes another that brings forth their murderous character. A man planted a vineyard, raised a wall around it, dug a pit for the winepress and built a watchtower. Then he rented it to some farmers and went away on a journey. At harvest he sent a servant to collect some of the fruit of the vineyard, but they seized him, beat him and sent him away empty-handed. Then he sent another servant whom they struck on the head and treated shamefully. He sent still another and that one they killed. He sent many others, some of them they beat, and others they killed.

He had a son, whom he loved. He sent him last of all, saying,

'They will respect my son.'

But the tenants said to one another, 'This is the heir. Come, let's kill him and the inheritance will be ours.' So they took him and killed him, and threw him out of the vineyard.

"Therefore when the owner of the vineyard comes, what will he do to these tenants?"

"He will bring those wretches to a wretched end," they replied. "And he will rent the vineyard to other tenants, who will give him his share of crop at harvest."

Jesus told them, "Have you never read in the Scriptures:
The stone the builders rejected
has become the cornerstone;
The Lord has done this,
and it is marvellous in our eyes.

"Therefore I tell you that the kingdom of God will be taken away from you and given to a people who will produce its fruit. He who falls on this stone will be broken to pieces, but he on whom it falls will be crushed."

The Jewish leaders knew the parable weaved around them and that the import of the message is as a nation they are guilty of rejecting the Cornerstone. But this stone grinds and breaks its foes, is a subtle warning yet to dawn on them.

Again he spoke to them in parables. The kingdom of heaven is like a king who prepared a wedding banquet for his son. He sent word to those invited that the banquet is ready that they may come and attend. But they refused.

Then he sent more servants with the royal message: 'My oxen and fattened cattle have been butchered, and everything is ready. Come to the banquet'.

But they paid little attention and went their way, one to his field and another to his business. The rest seized the servants, mistreated them and killed them. Enraged, the king sent his army and destroyed those murderers and burnt their city.

Then the king said to the servants, 'The banquet is ready, but those invited did not deserve to come. Go to the street corners and invite anyone you find. So the servants went out into the streets and gathered all they could find, both good and bad, and the wedding hall was filled with guests.

When the king came to see the guests, he noticed a man wearing no wedding clothes. 'Friend, how did you get in here?' the king asked, and the man was speechless.

Then the king ordered his attendants to tie him hand and foot, and throw him outside, into the darkness, where there will be weeping and gnashing of teeth.

"For many are invited, but few are chosen."

Juxtapose the second parable of the stubborn refusal of Israel and the third parable declaring the kingdom of God is open to all humanity — beyond culture, race and ideology. See how the two are interlinked; the former is Israel's history recapitulated in parable and the latter a kingdom principle and an idea whose time has come. The tragic story of Israel is a grim reminder of the consequences of stubborn refusal of God. Second Chronicle 36:15-16 pithily describes the wayward behaviour of Israel on the eve of the captivity of Judah, one of the divided kingdom, into Babylon.

"The Lord, the God of their fathers, sent word to them through his messengers again and again, because he had pity on his people and on his dwelling place. But they mocked God's messengers, despised his words and scoffed at his prophets until the wrath of the Lord was aroused against his people and there was no remedy."

Another passage, Numbers 14: 21-23, records the judgement of the Lord against his people:

"Nevertheless, as surely as I live and as surely as the glory of the Lord fills the whole earth, not one of the men who saw my glory and the miraculous signs I performed in Egypt and in the desert but who disobeyed me and tested me ten times — not one of them will ever see the land I promised on oath to their forefathers. No one who has treated me with contempt will ever see it."

The miraculous escape of their ancestors from Egypt, God's wonderful provision of manna, meat and water in the desert, and His supernatural presence in clouds during day and in the pillar of fire during night to protect and guide them, have not enhanced their faith. Because of their disbelief and scepticism, their forefathers wandered in the desert for forty years; because of idolatry the kingdom of Israel disappeared into Assyrian captivity in 721 BC; and because of backsliding the kingdom of Judah was wallowed by Babylonian in 587 BC. Back in their own homeland in 535 BC, the Jewish nation is on the verge of disappearing into a two millennia Diaspora. The parable turned prophetic in 70 AD when the Roman emperor Titus razed to the ground the City of Jerusalem.

The king in the parable is God, and his son the Son of God; those invited the nation of Israel and those in the street the humanity. The interesting point to note is someone hoodwinked the guards and sneaked in without the wedding garment, supplied to every invitee at the entrance. Symbolically it stands for God's righteousness gifted to every believer who trusts in the atoning sacrifice of Jesus Christ. But someone entered the banquet hall with self-righteousness which does not measure up to God's standard and is caught by the Omniscient eye. Bound hand and foot, he was cast out into the darkness, which is outside of God.

The three parables in a sequence speak of the three steps into the kingdom: *Repentance* in the first parable, *a receptive heart* that is lacking in the second parable, and the *Righteousness* of the Son of God, given freely to all those who respond to God's invitation as seen in the third parable. And outside of the kingdom is darkness, the state and place reserved for those who willfully reject the truth of God.

BATTLE OF WITS

The Pharisees and the Herodians (loyalists of King Herod) decided to trap Jesus in word and charge him with treason to be handed over to the Romans. So they sent their acolytes to Jesus in the pretext of learning.

"Teacher, we know you are a man of integrity. You aren't swayed by men, because you pay no attention to who they are; but you teach the way of God in accordance with the truth. Is it right to pay taxes to Caesar or not? Should we pay or shouldn't we?"

Knowing their hypocrisy, Jesus asked, "Why are you trying to trap me? Bring me a coin and let me look at it." They brought the coin, and he asked them, "Whose portrait is this? And whose inscription?"

"Caesar's," they replied.

"Render unto Caesar what is Caesar's and unto God what is God's."

Amazed, they made a retreat.

None can fail to observe the insincere language of the Pharisees. They pretended they were troubled by the ethical question of paying taxes to Caesar. Their game was to trap Jesus between flagrant unpatriotism and treason. If he said do not pay taxes, he is already in their traps; and if he said do pay taxes, that would be the unmaking of the Messiah as he would become unpopular with the crowd. But his answer startled them and send them scurrying for cover.

The Pharisees, the Sadducees and the Herodians were the three groups active during the time of Jesus. The Pharisees and the Herodians veered round Jewish nationalism while the religion of the Sadducees was worldliness. A running battle between the Sadducees and the Pharisees made it imperative for the former to engage the Rabbi in a theological debate to score over their rivals. So they began:

"Moses wrote that if a man dies leaving behind his wife but no children, his brother should marry the widow and have children for the deceased brother. There were seven brothers among us, the first one married and died without children, the second one married and died without children, and likewise all the seven, and finally the woman, too, died. At the resurrection whose wife will she be, since all the seven married her?"

"You neither know the scriptures nor the power of God. When the dead rise, they will neither marry nor be given in marriage; they will be like the angels in heaven. Haven't you read in the scriptures that God told Moses at the burning bush, `I am the God of Abraham, the God of Isaac, and the God of Jacob? He is not the God of the dead, but of the living. "

The Sadducees were a pleasure-loving people who denied life after death. They believed in power, money and the good things of life — in a 'heaven here and now'. They counted God's blessings in terms of prosperity and looked down upon the poor as cursed. This philosophy influenced the common Jews so much that when Jesus said it is hard for the rich to enter the kingdom of God, the disciples marvelled who then could be saved. When Jesus said, "Blessed are the poor (in spirit)," they could not understand. They thought the rich are blessed; the self-assertive and self-centred are blessed.

Barbed sarcasm is the favourite weapon of the Sadducees and they use it skilfully under the veneer of sophistication to draw a laughter of derision from the audience. The Pharisees found them hard nuts to crack because they reckoned only the first five books of Moses called the Law and discounted the Prophets and the Wisdom literature. To prove the Sadducee wrong, the Pharisee must find apt verses only from Moses, which is a tough challenge. Nor are the debates devoid of high entertainments. Look at this anecdote. A man was induced to wed the twelve widows of his twelve brothers, each widow promising to pay for the expenses of one month, and the directing Rabbi for those of the 13th month. But to his horror, after three years the women returned, laden with thirty-six children, to claim the fulfilment of the Rabbis promise! Some Rabbis forbid a woman who has lost two husbands from marrying a third, and a woman who has lost three husbands from marrying a fourth, as there might be some fate connected with her. Thus from spirituality we enter the realm of superstition.

The defence of resurrection in those days laboured under two-fold difficulty: (i) The most well-attested Resurrection of Jesus Christ had not yet taken place, and (ii) the Old Testament's revelation on the subject were hazy. The Sadducee would demand proof in precise letter, not allusions like 'This people will rise up,' 'I kill and make alive' or visions like to valley of the dry bones.

The Pharisees' own half-baked ideas of after-life landed them in comical predicament. There were debates within the Pharisee circle itself on whether the dead will rise in their own clothes or naked. One Pharisee went to the extent of taking an analogy from the farm and said the grains are buried 'naked' but rise clothed, and hence the humans will certainly be clothed. One school of Pharisees argued that the dead will rise in their own body looking exactly as they were with all the physical deformities, like blindness, deafness, lameness. Another school argued that the pious of Israel would rise in the sacred soil of Palestine while others would have to roll through underground cavities till they reached the Holy Land to rise to newness of life. The Sadducees could not have chosen a better topic than Resurrection — the gold mine of confusion where quibblers and circumlocuters had a field day.

Christ meets their challenge squarely because of who he is. His authentic assertion that the children of Resurrection are like angels settled the issue. They have a different type of body called glorified body and do not marry or are given in marriage. These glorified 'bodies' are beyond time, space and matter, and could pass through walls and fortresses, and could become visible and invisible in a fraction of a second. They would be modelled on the prototype of Christ's Resurrected (spiritual) body.

His scriptural exposition on the revelation to Moses that God calls Himself the God of Abraham, Isaac and Jacob, their patriarchal fathers, more than meets Sadducees' demand for precision. Their veneration of Moses and the illustration from the heart of the text silences them.

Christ now goes to the root of their ambivalence — the lack of knowledge of the word of God and the power of God, one leading to the other. So powerful was the impact on the audience that in the silence that ensued, a Pharisee walked up to him to congratulate, "Teacher, thou has beautifully said."

The practice of marrying a brother's childless widow has fallen into discredit long before the time of Christ; but marrying for beauty and wealth did exist and one Rabbi forbade them both terming them incestuous. The Resurrection is the innermost shrine in the sanctuary of Christ's mission towards which he steadily moved, and the living cornerstone of the church he built and the spire, which points all men heavenward.

A teacher of the law, impressed by the answers Jesus gave, wanted to know which is the most important commandment of all.

"Hear, O Israel, the Lord our God, the Lord is one. Love the Lord your God with all your heart and with all your soul and with all your mind and with all your strength" is the most important one.

"Love your neighbour as yourself" is the second. When Jesus said, "On these two commandments hang all the Law and the

Prophets," this man began to see the exuding moral beauty of the Law. And the first commandment without the second would have been a theoretical abstraction.

Delighted, this man said these two commandments are more important than all burnt offerings and sacrifices.

Jesus commended his godly perception: "You are not far from the kingdom of God." When you seek God, the kingdom is near and when you find God you realize the kingdom is within you.

Some rabbinical schools teach that there are heavy and light commandments with greater and smaller rewards. They gave greater weight to tradition, which is a collection of rabbinical interpretations, than to the scriptures themselves. Thus the Law meant to communicate God's holiness became a labyrinth of burdensome rules for the people, which the Pharisees escaped through the legal loopholes.

Now Jesus asks a question to the teachers of the Law:

Speaking in the Holy Spirit, David declared, "The Lord said to my Lord: Sit at my right hand until I put your enemies under your feet. David himself calls him `Lord'. How then can he be his son?"

No one answered, no one seems to know except the Son of David. What else should David call God who took human form and was born in a manger in Bethlehem, but the Lord?

WOE TO YOU PHARISEES!

Jesus began his preaching ministry by proclaiming the beatitudes (blessings) in the Sermon on the Mount and ends it by proclaiming woes on the Scribes and the Pharisees whose interpretation of the Law turned the nation of Israel spiritually blind.

The teachers of the Law and the Pharisees sit in Moses' seat. So you must obey them and do everything they tell you. But do not do what they do, for they do not practise what they preach.

Everything they do is done for men to see: They make their phylacteries wide and the tassels on their garments long; they love the place of honour at banquets and the most important seats in the synagogues; they love to be greeted in the market places and to have men call them Rabbi.

But you are not to be called Rabbi, for you have only one Master and you are all brothers. And do not call anyone on earth Father, for you have one Father, and he is in heaven. Nor are you to be called teacher, for you have one Teacher, the Christ. The greatest among you will be your servant. For whoever exalts himself will be humbled, and whoever humbles himself will be exalted.

Jesus begins his denunciation with a vivid portrayal of the Pharisee, who loves to be called 'Rabbi, Father and Teacher'. He is not forbidding anyone calling his father, Father or his teacher, Teacher or his master, Rabbi. But he reminds them that the true Father, Teacher and Rabbi is God himself and men ought to treat each other as brothers. He also warns against self-exultation that will lead to humiliation and exhorts them to be truly humble to be exalted (by God).

Woe to you, teachers of the law and Pharisees, you hypocrites! You shut the kingdom of heaven in men's faces. You yourself do not enter nor will you let those enter who are trying to.

Woe to you, teachers of the law and Pharisees, you hypocrites! You travel over land and sea to win a single convert, and when he becomes one, you make him twice as much a son of hell as you are.

Woe to you, blind guides! You say, 'If anyone swears by the temple, it means nothing; but if anyone swears by the gold of the temple, he is bound by the oath.' You blind fools! Which is greater: the gold, or the temple that makes the gold sacred. You also say, 'If anyone swears by the altar, it means nothing; but if anyone swears by the gift on it, he is bound by the oath.' You blind men! Which is greater: the gift or the altar that makes the gift sacred. Therefore, he who swears by the altar swears by it and by everything on it. And he who swears by the temple swears by it and by the one who dwells in it. And he who swears by heaven swears by God's throne and by the one who sits on it.

Woe to you, teachers of the law and Pharisees, you hypocrites! You give a tenth of your spices — mint, dill and cummin. But you have neglected the more important matters of the law — justice, mercy and faithfulness. You should have practised the latter, without neglecting the former. You blind guides! You strain out a gnat but swallow a camel.

Woe to you, teachers of the law and Pharisees, you hypocrites! You clean the outside of the cup and dish, but inside they are full of greed and self-indulgence. Blind Pharisee! First clean the inside of the cup and dish, and then the outside also will be clean.

Woe to you, teachers of the law and Pharisees, you hypocrites! You are like whitewashed tombs, which look beautiful on the outside but on the inside are full of dead men's bones and everything unclean. In the same way, on the outside you appear to people as righteous but on the inside you are full of hypocrisy and wickedness.

Woe to you, teachers of the law and Pharisees, you hypocrites! You build tombs for the prophets and decorate the graves of the righteous. And you say, 'If we had lived in the days of our fathers, we would not have taken part with them in shedding the blood of the prophets. So you testify against yourself that you are the descendants of those who murdered the prophets. Fill up then the measure of the sin of your forefathers!

You snakes! You brood of vipers! How will you escape being condemned to hell? Therefore, I am sending you prophets and wise men and teachers. Some of them you will kill and crucify, others you will flog in your synagogues and pursue from town to town. And so upon you will be all the righteous blood that has been shed on earth from the blood of righteous Abel to the blood of Zechariah son of Berekiah, whom you murdered between the temple and the altar. I tell you the truth, all this will come upon this generation.

O Jerusalem, Jerusalem, you who kill the prophets and stone those sent to you, how often I have longed to gather your children together as a hen gathers her chicks under her wings, but you were not willing. Look, your house is left desolate. For I tell you, you will not see me again until you say, 'Blessed is he who comes in the name of the Lord.'

Now the reasons for the **eight-fold denunciations** of woe which is the outpouring of his holy wrath:

1. They shut the kingdom of God against the people because of their opposition to Christ. Had they taught the Scriptures instead of man-made tradition, Israel would have recognised the Messiah of the scriptures, to whom they sang hosanna. The Pharisees are exclusively responsible for rejecting the Messiah.

2. They are covetous hypocrites who have fraudulent minds.

Their long prayers to be seen of men and exploitation of widow's homes for profit betray their duplicity.

3. They convert to make people two-fold children of hell.
4. They are morally blind and profane; devalue the name of God in teaching men that the gold in the altar is more precious than the sovereignty and holiness of God.
5. They tithe even in the smallest of things, but forget justice, mercy and love.
6. They clean the outside but, alas, not the inside.
7. They are rotten within, totally corrupt.
8. Their hands have shed blood, martyrs' blood. Two centuries and a half ago, Priest Zechariah was stoned, by the king's command, in the court of the temple, whose blood did not dry up, as legends have it, till Nebuzar-adam entered the temple and avenged it.

"O Jerusalem, Jerusalem, ... how often I have longed to gather your children, as a hen gathers her chicks under her wings." The godly character of Jesus pour forth in his longing love for his people to protect them under his Sheikinah glory. God loves His creation — especially the crown of his creation, man — and He longs for the love of His creation. But to trample His love is to invite judgement.

Till you say, 'Blessed is he who comes in the name of the Lord, you shall see me no more.' And with these words, he walks out of the temple that will be desolate for centuries to come.

Good deeds seldom escape the eye of Jesus: a poor widow put two copper coins into the treasury box and Jesus sitting across remarked, "This poor widow has put more into the treasury than all the others. They all gave out of their wealth, but she, out of her poverty, put in everything — all she had to live on."

SERMON ON RESURRECTION

Some Hellenistic Jews sought an audience with Jesus; they met Philip who took them to Andrew and the two together took them to Jesus. They had come to Jerusalem for the Passover.

"The hour has come for the Son of Man to be glorified. I tell you the truth, unless a kernel of wheat falls to the ground and dies, it remains only a single seed. But if it dies, it produces many seeds. The man who loves his life will lose it, while the man who hates his life in this world will keep it for eternal life. Whoever serves me must follow me; and where I am, my servant also will be. My Father will honour the one who serves me."

That was the shortest sermon on resurrection — life through death, and the multiplication of faith from one life to many. Those who esteem their biological life more than their spiritual life may lose the latter; and those who sacrifice their biological life for the kingdom may draw many more lives to God. A life that loves God is a life that serves God is a life that God honours with eternal life.

"Now my heart is troubled, and what shall I say? `Father save me from this hour?' No it was for this very reason I came to this hour. Father, glorify your name!"

Then a voice came from heaven, "I have glorified it, and glorify it again." Those standing by thought it thundered; some said an angel spoke to him. At his baptism in Jordan, the heaven was opened and those around heard a voice from heaven; at the Mount of Transfiguration, once more the heaven was opened and the disciples with him heard a voice from heaven. And a third time now, the heaven was opened and those around him heard a voice from heaven. His baptism of fire is about to begin; and the prayers of those who live close to heaven are answered instantly.

"This voice was for your benefit, not mine. Now is the time for judgement on this world; now the prince of this world will be driven out. But I, when I am lifted up from the earth, will draw all men to myself."

Truth and illusion are poles apart; while illusion leads to disillusionment, truth leads to eternal life. The world cannot escape judgement, drifting between truth and illusion. Satan who deceives people through illusions will be cast into the Lake of Fire, from where there is no escape. And Christ, after his resurrection, will draw humanity to himself — in all ages, cultures and geographic zones.

THE SECOND COMING

As they were leaving the temple, one of the disciples marvelled, "Look teacher! What massive stones! What magnificent buildings!" Indeed, the temple of Herod the Great was awe-inspiring. That half-Jew spent a fortune building it to win the loyalty of his subjects and the enterprise took 40 years — still not complete during the time of Jesus. To the prescient eye of the Son of God, it was a building in ruins, razed to the ground by the Romans in 70 AD. "Not one stone will be left on another; everyone will be thrown down," he prophesied.

While Jesus was sitting on Mount Olives overlooking the temple, Peter, James, John and Andrew asked him privately, "Tell us when will these things happen, and what will be the sign of your coming and the end of the age?"

"Watch out that no one deceives you. For many will come in my name claiming, `I am the Christ' and deceive many. You will hear of wars and rumours of war, but see to it that you are not alarmed. Such things must happen, but the end is still to come. Nation will rise against nation, and kingdom against kingdom. There will be famines and earthquakes in various places. All these things are the beginning of birth pains.

"Before all this, they will lay hands on you and persecute you. They will deliver you to synagogues and prisons, and you will be brought before kings and governors, and all on account of my name. Do not worry before hand how you will defend yourselves. For I will give you words and wisdom that none of your adversaries will be able to resist or contradict. You will be betrayed even by parents, brothers, relatives and friends, and they will put some of you to death. All men will hate you because of me. By standing firm you will gain life. Because of increase in wickedness, the love of many will grow cold."

The destruction of the temple and the Second Coming are two events far distant in time, though the disciples may have misunderstood it as the one super-imposing on the other. The message becomes clearer when the two are seen as separate landmarks.

Since deception will grow into a major industry in religion, disciples in all ages have been warned to guard against it. False Christs have appeared before and since Jesus Christ and deceived many. But the end of Age would come as a political, economic and social catastrophe preceded by a love-death since people will grow cold for the violence and wickedness all around. And the persecution of Christians witnessed in the early centuries will be revived.

"When you see Jerusalem surrounded by armies, you will know that its desolation is near. For this is the time of punishment in fulfilment of all that has been written. How dreadful it will be for pregnant women and nursing mothers! There will be great distress in the land and wrath against this people. They will fall by the sword and will be taken as prisoners to all the nations. Jerusalem will be trampled on by the gentiles until the times of the gentiles are fulfilled."

This prophecy was fulfilled in 70 AD but the final battle of Armageddon prophesied to be fought in and around this region opens up possibilities of multiple fulfilment. Considering the gentiles still occupy part of Jerusalem, the danger is real.

"After the distress of those days, the sun will be darkened, and the moon will not give light; and the stars will fall from the sky and the heavenly bodies will be shaken."

"And the sign of the Son of Man will appear in the sky, and

all the nations of the earth will mourn. They will see the Son of Man coming on the clouds of the sky with power and great glory. And he will send his angels with a loud trumpet call, and they will gather his elect from the four winds, from one end of the heavens to the other."

A nuclear holocaust or a cosmic cataclysm will literally fulfil the prophesy with the sun and the moon invisible to the hapless survivors on earth because of thick, black smoke that envelope the atmosphere and stars falling from the galaxy because of the dazed state of the inhabitants and the optical illusion that abet their vision. And the Son of Man will appear in the clouds in the full view of humanity, in all power and glory to judge the living and the dead who will rise again.

Like lightning from the heavens, the Son of God will appear swiftly unexpectedly. As in the days of Noah, people will be busy eating, drinking, marrying and giving in marriage and laughing at the righteous till suddenly their laughter turned panic.

THE LAST PARABLES

The disciples ought to live in a state of perpetual readiness. To illustrate the point Jesus told them a parable. Ten virgins went out with lamps to meet the bridegroom. Five of them were wise and took a can of oil with them; five were foolish, so foolish that they did not take oil but the lamp.

The bridegroom was delayed and the virgins fell asleep. At midnight, they heard a voice, 'The bridegroom is coming; go out and meet him.' The foolish virgins suddenly discovered their total lack of preparedness and pleaded with the wise to share their oil. Being wise, they replied, 'Neither we nor you will then have enough. Why don't you go to the market and buy for yourself?' In the meantime, the bridegroom came and in went the wise virgins.

When the foolish virgins returned, the door of opportunity was already closed; they knocked, but were told by none less than the groom, 'I do not know you'.

Today thousands of people perilously live without knowing God. Today is the day of opportunity; tomorrow the door of grace may be closed. Then all that remains is judgement — banishment from God's presence, which the foolish virgins faced.

The kingdom of God is not a kingdom of laziness but of enterprise, where each one multiplies one's talent for the glory of the king. Jesus told the parable of a man who went on a long journey after distributing his money among his three servants according to their ability. To the first one he gave five talents, the second two and the third one. When he returned after a long while, he called the servants to account.

The first one said, "Sir, you gave me five talents, I have made five more talents."

"Well done, good and faithful servant! You have been faithful with a few things; I will put you in charge of many things. Come and share your master's happiness!"

The man with two talents also came. "Sir, you have entrusted me with two talents; see I have made two more."

"Well done, good and faithful servant! You have been faithful with a few things; I will put you in change of many things. Come and share your master's happiness!"

Came the third servant and said, "Sir, I know that you are a hard man, harvesting where you have not sworn and gathering where you have not scattered seed. So I was afraid and hid your talent in the ground."

"You wicked and slothful servant. You should have put the money with the bankers so that when I return, I would have collected with interest."

And the master said, "Take away the talent from him and give it to the one who has ten talents. Now throw that worthless servant outside, into the darkness, where there will be weeping and gnashing of teeth." There is reward for enterprise and loyalty, punishment for sloth.

The last three parables of Jesus Christ are devoted to divine judgement, and the last one is exclusively devoted to the Last Judgement. The setting is the Great White Throne.

The Son of Man comes in all his glory and sits on the throne judging the nations — separating the righteous from the wicked as a shepherd would the sheep from the goat.

He tells those on his right: "Come, you blessed of my Father; take the inheritance prepared for you since the creation of the world. For I was hungry and you gave me something to eat, I was thirsty and you gave me something to drink, I was a stranger and you invited me in, I was naked and you clothed me, I was sick and you looked after me, I was in prison and you came to visit me."

Then the righteous will answer, "When did we see you hungry, when did we see you thirsty, when did we see you a stranger, when did we see you naked, when did we see you sick, when did we see you in prison?"

"I tell you the truth, whatever you have done for the least of my brothers, you have done for me."

Then he turns to those on his left:

"Depart from me, you cursed, into the eternal fire prepared for the devil and his angels. For I was hungry and you gave me nothing to eat, I was thirsty and you gave me nothing to drink, I was a stranger and you did not invite me in, I was naked you did not clothe me, I was sick and in prison and you did not look after me."

Then they will go away to eternal punishment and the righteous to eternal life.

The priceless beauty of the last parable is that it defines the criteria for heaven. It is a measure of godliness in a person, reflected in his love and compassion for others — not religiosity, as the neo-Pharisees would love to have it. And hell is too real to be scoffed off as the last three parables warn us in metaphoric terms as darkness outside or eternal fire.

The three parables teach that the kingdom is relationship (with God), the kingdom is (spiritual) enterprise and the kingdom is of loving hearts.

The Passover is just two days away as Jesus reminds his disciples, the day when the Son of Man will be betrayed, and handed over to the chief priests and Jewish leaders, and finally to the Romans and to be crucified.

Even as Jesus was telling his disciples of what lies ahead, the chief priests and Jewish leaders were plotting for his arrest — "nevertheless, not on a festival day" to avoid popular uprising, they said. Events were moving to a climax.

Book Six

THE PASSOVER LAMB

A terrified Pharaoh decreed freedom to his bonded labour Israel after the angel of death struck down the eldest sons of the land. Deep within the psyche of the nation Israel grew the conviction that it was the blood of the Lamb sprinkled by their forefathers that saved them from the angel of death. In some mysterious way the blood of the Lamb they sacrificed since prefigured the blood of Christ to be shed in that Passover season.

To commemorate this historic day, the Jewish diaspora would converge at Jerusalem. They made new friends and revisited their kindred in Judea and Galilee, studying their roots. In that season, every Jew considered himself privileged to belong to God's chosen race; and the topic of discussion in religious circles for one month centered on the Passover.

The Jewish month Nissan roughly corresponds to April and on the evening of 13th Nissan began the week-long Passover feast. For the Jew that is 14th Nissan because he reckoned the day from evening to evening. The feast of unleavened bread — leaven stands for hypocrisy, malice and deception — started with a solemn search of the house, the inmates holding lighted candles and looking for any leaven that might have been hidden or fallen aside by accident.

In the province of Galilee, they abstained from work the whole day but in Judea work ceased only at noon. An hour before noon marked the forbidden time for eating anything that was leavened. The pious stopped eating leavened food even at 10 am, an hour before the forbidden time. As a public notification, two desecrated thank offering cakes were kept on a bench in the temple; the removal of one indicated the time for eating leavened bread had passed and the removal of the other proclaimed the time for destroying all leaven had come.

Jesus sends Peter and John to prepare the Passover meal, probably after the removal of the first cake in the temple. The venue remains a mystery but a sign is given that they will see a man carrying a pitcher — an unusual sight in Palestine where women carried water. Follow him to the house he enters and tell the master of the house, "The Teacher asks: Where is the guest room where I may eat the Passover with my disciples? He will show you a large upper room, all furnished. Make preparations there."

This meal is so very special to the Master that he says, "With desire I have desired to eat this Passover with you before I suffer." The Lord does not want any introducers to break in and disturb the solemnity of the occasion — least of all a betrayal scene that Judas would stage shortly. Therefore the venue is kept a mystery for the ten while Peter and John are led to the Upper Room, which John Mark's father owns and which is not far from the Chief Priest's. Jesus asks only for a small room, something like a manger (as the Greek word *katalyma* suggests) but the owner of the mansion — presumably a follower of Jesus — offered the most spacious Upper Room meant for special guests. This room, like all guestrooms of upper middle class homes, has a separate entrance and exit stairs independent of the living room.

In Jerusalem, no Jew considers his house his own during the Passover season. John Mark's father made all provisions for the meal — wine, unleavened bread and even bitter herbs — except the Paschal Lamb and the festive sacrifice (Chagigah) to supplement it for a larger number of partakers. Bitter herbs come in five varieties to be dipped in salt water or vinegar and later in a mixture (Charoseth) made of nuts, raisins, apples and almonds. The red wine is diluted in water in one: two ratio to prevent anyone getting drunk.

While Peter and John were preparing the meal, things were

happening in another part of Jerusalem. Judas who carried the purse must have bought the lamb on Wednesday afternoon. From the sheep market he would have gone to the temple to get the lamb inspected and there learned about the Sanhedrine in session discussing how to get rid of Jesus.

Reading together the accounts of St. Luke and St. Mathew, one gets the nearest picture of what transpired that Wednesday afternoon.

"Then Satan entered Judas, called Iscariot, one of the Twelve. And Judas went to the chief priests and the officers of the temple guard and discussed with them how he might betray Jesus. They were delighted and agreed to give him money. He consented and watched for an opportunity to hand Jesus over to them when no crowd was present." (St. Luke 22:3-6).

"Then one of the Twelve – the one called Judas Iscariot – went to the chief priests and asked, 'What are you willing to give me if I hand him over to you?' So they counted out for him thirty silver coins. From then on Judas watched for an opportunity to hand him over." (St. Matthew 26:14-16).

St. Luke captures the spiritual dimension while St. Matthew the monetary dimension. To be sure, Judas came back richer and with his mask intact.

Alfred Edersheim describes the temple scenes thus:

At half past three would begin the normal evening sacrifice and the evening prayer an hour before. But on the Passover day the prayer would begin an hour earlier than before. Around one o' clock the two disciples must be climbing the hill of the temple of Jerusalem, mingling with the pilgrims and their sacrifices. There is jubilation all around, but loneliness and sorrow in the heart of the two disciples.

White-robed Priests and Levites packed the Priest's Court with all their 24 divisions in attendance. Psalm 81 was sung in three sections broken three times by the three-fold blast from the silver trumpets of the Priests. Before burning the incense for the evening sacrifice and lamps in the golden candlestick were trimmed, the Paschal Lambs were slain.

The pilgrims were admitted into the court of priest's in three batches. When the first batch entered, the massive gates made of nicanor leading from the court of women into the court of Israel were closed. The side gates to the Court of Priests too were closed. A three-fold blast from the Priest's trumpets proclaimed that the Paschal Lambs were being slain.

Every Israelite slew the lamb for himself and the officiating Priests in two rows stood by the great Altar of Burnt Offering. One caught up the blood from the dying lamb in a golden bowel and handed it to his fellow-Priest receiving in return an empty bowl after it was jerked in one jet at the base of the altar.

Meanwhile, the Levites chanted Hallel and only the first line of every Psalm was repeated by the congregation while to every other line they responded with Hallelujah till Psalm cxviii was reached. Then besides the first, these three lines were repeated:

Save now, I beseech Thee, Lord;

O Lord, I beseech Thee, send now prosperity.

Blessed be He that cometh in the Name of the Lord.

As Peter and John sang these lines, the scenes of the triumphal entry and the shouting of the frenzied crowd, 'Blessed is he who comes in the name of the Lord' must have engaged their mind.

Flayed and cleansed, the sacrificial lamb was laid on the staves which rested on the shoulders of Peter and John. Those parts which were to be burnt on the altar were removed and prepared for burning. Now they wind their way back to the Upper Room. The lamb was roasted on a pomegranate spit that passed right through it from mouth to vent. While roasting care was taken that the lamb did not get burnt touching the oven. Finally, everything was ready and only the festive lamps remained to be set.

The dazzling beauty of the gorgeous temple built with snow-white marble and gold glittering in the sun would fill the visitors with awe. The smoke was rising from the Altar of the Burnt Offering; and in the real sense, it was the last time the Pascal Lambs need to be sacrificed. The true Pascal Lamb who would take away the sin of the world is meandering his way to the Passover meal to annul all animal sacrifices and open the door to a New and Living Way. That was the last sunset Jesus would see before his death; descending over Mount Olives into the Holy City, pilgrims carrying Passover lambs on their shoulders passed by the true Passover Lamb. As the first three stars appeared the silver trumpets of the temple proclaimed once more the arrival of the Pascha.

The public ministry of Jesus began with a sacrament and ended with a sacrament — his baptism and the Lord's Supper. Both the sacraments are linked to his death and resurrection. In baptism, the believer identifies himself with the life of Christ, is buried with Him, and rises again with Him spiritually while in the Lord's Supper we remember his death and resurrection till He comes again.

As far as we can see, this is the only sacrifice Jesus offered once for all, says Alfred Edersheim. Before his public ministry Jesus could have attended any of the Passovers but he would then be the guest and not the head of a company which must consist of at least 10 persons. As for the three Passovers during his ministry, in the first the Apostles were not gathered, in the second he was in the utter most parts of Galilee in the borderland of Tyre and Sidon where no sacrifice could be brought. Therefore, this was the first and only sacrifice Jesus offered.

The trouble began right at the outset — who is the greatest among them? The greatest should sit next to Christ in the kingdom and at the Passover table. The Pharisees settled their rank by virtue of education, age and social standing but the disciples could not agree on a norm. The man from Kerioth could have started the trouble by cornering a seat close to Christ and perhaps that ought to have been Peter's. Placed with the responsibility of keeping the table, Peter was clearly out manoeuvred in the musical chair where each one tried to grab the best seat for oneself. With none of the contenders willing to vacate the seat they grabbed, Peter thought it fit to take a seat of lesser honour in the true spirit of the Sermon on the Mount. Notwithstanding Leonado da Vinci's immortal painting of the Last Supper, the Jews reclined around a long rectangular table facing each other in two opposite rows and a perpendicular row at one end joining the two.

The gospel accounts agree that Judas was sitting close to Jesus so that he could give the bread (sop) dipped in the dish without stretching his hand or passing it on. And when Jesus whispered to Judas, "Do what you do quickly," no one else except John possibly could hear it.

To betray one's own Master, one must be the worst specimen of a human being. "And during supper, the devil having already cast it into his heart, that Judas Iscariot, the son of Simon, shall betray him," explains St John. Judas is possessed by Satan, who controls him through his love of money. Satan wherever present manifests his character and you often find the disciples quarrelling because of the influence of the man of sin.

The Paschal supper begins with the Head of the company taking the first cup of wine with Thanksgiving. Then comes two benedictions, the first over the wine and the second for the return of the day, implying God preserve them for the next Passover. "Blessed art Thou Jehovah our God, who has created the fruit of the Vine!" Thus goes the first benediction, after which the cup of wine is passed around with these words, "No more I drink the cup of wine with you until we meet in the kingdom."

Now comes the washing of hands when the Head of the company would rise and go to each member and washes his/her hands. The washing of hands is observed twice, first soon after the first cup and second much later but before the actual meal (on the lamb) and by everyone present.

Jesus turns this ceremonial washing of hands into the emblem of practical Christianity: The Master washing the feet of the disciples, signifying the essence of Christianity is service to humanity. If only the disciples of later centuries practised it, there would have been no schisms within the church.

The washing of the feet had an electrifying impact on the disciples in the background of their petty squabbling. St. John pictorially captures the moment.

He got up from the meal, took off his outer clothing, and wrapped a towel around his waist. Then he poured water into the basin and began to wash his disciples' feet, drying them with the towel that is wrapped around him.

When the Lord came to Simon Peter, he asked in disbelief, "Lord, are you going to wash my feet?" The question suggests he was the first of the disciples whose feet Jesus washed.

"You do not realise now what I am doing, but later you will understand."

"You shall never wash my feet," Peter insisted.

"Unless I wash you, you have no part with me."

"Then, Lord, not just my feet but my hands and my head as well," Peter replied, because he likes to have a share more than others,

"A person who has had a bath needs only to wash his feet; his body is clean. And you are clean though not every one of you."

When Jesus had finished washing their feet, he put on his outer garment and returned to his place. "Do you understand what I have done for you? You call me teacher and Lord, and rightly so, for that is what I am. Now that I, your Lord and teacher, have washed your feet, you also should wash one another's feet. I have set you an example that you should do as I have done for you."

Christian leadership is one of setting examples but one who is not clean has no part in the ministry of Christ as the story of Judas would tell.

After the washing of hand, dishes are placed on the table; the Head of the company dips some of the bitter herbs into vinegar (or salt-water), says a blessing, partakes of them and passes on to each member. Then he breaks one of the unleavened cakes, half of which is put aside for after-supper or desert (Aphiqomon) which served as the bread of the Holy Eucharist. The dish with the first half of the unleavened cake – called the Bread of Misery — is now raised with these words, "This is the bread of misery which our fathers ate in the land of Egypt. All that are hungry, come and eat; all that are needy, come, keep the Pascha."

On this the second cup is filled, and the youngest member of the company will make a formal inquiry on the meaning of all the observances of that night, and the head of the company will give a discourse on the significance of the events of the First Passover. Then the cup is raised a second time with special prayers. After the reading of the first two Psalms called Hallel, the cup is raised a third time with prayers and the cup drank. Thus ends the first part of the service.

Now begins the Paschal meal by all washing their hands as part of the ritual. The supper itself begins with eating a piece of unleavened cake, then of the bitter herbs dipped in charoseth, and lastly two small pieces of unleavened cake, between which a piece of bitter radish is placed. The sop which the head of the company gives to everyone consists flesh of the Paschal Lamb, a piece of unleavened bread and bitter herbs.

Notwithstanding what Judas was about to do, Jesus loved him to the end and gave him the last opportunity to repent. "One of you who dip his finger in my cup will betray me," Jesus said inviting a possible confession. On hearing this the disciples were exceedingly sorrowful and Peter bitten by the curiosity bug beckoned John who was leaning on the breast of his Master to ask, 'Who is that man?' Everyone in the company started asking, "Is it I Lord?" Then came Judas' turn to ask. Even as he was asking, Jesus said, "It is the one to whom I give the sop." And he dipped the sop in the dish and handed it over to Judas. "What you are about to do, do it quickly", Jesus told him. Judas misses the last opportunity, takes the sop and eats it. And into the night he walks, into the night of his life.

"The Son of Man goes as it is written but woe unto the man who betrays him; it was better for him that he was not born at all." Jesus was speaking in the full knowledge of the judgement to come on this son of perdition.

No one knew where Judas was going. The other disciples thought he was sent on a special mission because each one of them received a sop dipped in the dish as was the practice after Judas received the first sop. When Judas whispered, "Is it I Rabbi" into his Master's ear, "Yes," said Jesus so gently that no one else could hear. Even in their wildest imagination they could not believe he would turn out to be a traitor. But having sold himself to the Devil to betray his Master for 30 silver coins there was no turning back for Judas.

The traitor departed (read Satan departed) and left alone with his disciples, Jesus opened up his heart. St Luke captures the mood of the moment: "With desire I have desired to eat this Passover with you before I suffer. For I tell you I will not eat it again until it finds fulfillment in the kingdom of God." (St Luke 22:15-16) One can see the seeking love of God and His longing love to transport the disciples to a higher realm of holiness befitting communion with God.

After taking the cup he gave thanks and said, "Take this and divide it among you. For I tell you I will not drink again of the fruit of the vine until the kingdom of God comes."

And he took the bread, gave thanks and broke it, and gave it to them, saying, "This is my body given for you; do this in remembrance of me." The remembrance of the *past*, the fellowship of the *present* and the reality of the kingdom in the *future* are symbolically fused into the very person of Jesus Christ through this deed.

In the same way, after the supper he took the cup, saying,

"This is the new covenant in my blood, which is poured out for you (for the remission of sins)."

That was the true meaning of the New Passover, of which the old was a mere prefigure. For centuries the Jews had been sacrificing the Passover Lamb but the faithful among them were looking for the true Passover Lamb to come. The New Covenant (New Testament) is an agreement between God and man written in the blood of Christ. It is the blood shed for the forgiveness of the sin of mankind and to restore the broken communion with God.

"Now is the Son of Man glorified and God is glorified in him. If God is glorified in him, God will glorify the Son in himself, and will glorify him at once." In accomplishing human redemption, the Son of man is glorified; and the Father is glorified because it was the Father's plan and the Father in turn will crown his Son with glory — the glory that he had before he took human form.

"My children, I will be with you only a little longer. Where I am going, you cannot come." Jesus is going to be with the Father and the disciples will have to tarry a little longer to be with him again.

"A new commandment I give you: Love one another. As I have loved you, so you must love one another. By this all men will know that you are my disciples, if you love one another." True love is the most difficult to practise in a competitive world running after material acquisitions. In no uncertain terms, Jesus declared love is the hallmark of true discipleship.

"Lord, where are you going?" Peter asked.

"Where I am going you cannot follow now, but you will follow later."

Peter is asking for trouble. "Lord, why can't I follow you now? I will lay down my life for you." Jesus came to lay down his life for Peter and the whole world. Like the other eleven, Peter was yet to grasp the meaning of the word gospel. "Will you really lay down your life for me? I tell you the truth, before the rooster crows, you will disown me three times." Simon exudes confidence in the flesh which will certainly invite spiritual disasters. Simon's illustration should deter every believer from putting confidence in the flesh.

At the close of the supper, the third cup is filled — which St Paul calls the Cup of Blessing — with special blessings pronounced. It was the custom after meal to break and partake of the after-dish which corresponds to the Lord's Supper. One cannot be certain how much of the Paschal rituals were observed in the Upper Room since the gospel writers are silent on this. But it is safe to assume that the broad features with which the disciples are familiar must have been observed and that the Lord's Supper followed the Paschal meal.

"The Lord's Supper the eternal presence of the living God for the empowerment and enrichment of the believer. He who partakes, partakes in the eternal presence of the Lord. It is a spiritual mystery to be experienced not explained, and he who takes from us our mystery takes from us our sacrament," says Prof. Duncan (J) of Edinburgh.

The cup is filled a fourth time and the remaining part of the Halel is sung. Alfred Edershein argues that the Farewell Discourse and the High Priestly Prayer that follow the Lord's Supper could scarcely have been on the narrow streets leading to Kidron because they were too narrow to hold an assembly of twelve and hence must be in the Upper Room itself.

THE TROUBLED HEARTS

The last words of great men have a ring of eternal truth that are apt to be revisited time and again. The last book of your favourite author, the last speech of your favourite leader, the last performance of your favourite singer or actor, the last words of your dying father or mother or the last letter of a very special friend touches your life deeper. The farewell discourse of Jesus Christ has been the subject of meditation down the ages.

"Let not your heart be troubled," begins the famous discourse quintessential for Christian living. Troubled hearts are symptomatic of weak faith or shaken faith. The right solution for troubled hearts is to go to the Maker and Healer of hearts. Therefore Jesus says, "Trust in God, trust also in me." To trust God is to hand over the reigns of your life to Him so that He can order your life. When God is truly the centre of your being, He stills the storms of your life, as Jesus demonstrated at the Lake of Galilee when the disciples were out of their wits caught in the squall.

Satan — God's adversary and evil personified — normally peddles in two areas of human weakness: fear and doubt. He will either try to frighten you or cast darts of scepticism in your mind, both of which lead to turbulence. Satan himself exists by denying his existence so that you don't doubt his presence or his stratagem. The key to overcoming Satan is to trust God and trust the word of God.

"In my Father's house are many mansions; if it were not so, I would have told you. I am going there to prepare a place for you.

And if I go and prepare a place for you, I will come back and take you to be with me that you also may be where I am. You know the way to the place where I am going."

Heaven is a state of bliss and joy where no traces of tears and sorrow are found because it is a sinless zone. Through this imagery of spacious mansion, Jesus drives home the truth that beyond the veil of death is life and reality. Jesus did not reveal more on the life hereafter because of human scepticism.

As if enacting a divine script Thomas asks, "We don't know where you are going, then how do we know the way?" Jesus was setting the stage for the next phase of revelation: "I am the Way, the Truth and Life. No one comes to the Father except through me. If you really knew me, you would know my Father as well. From now on, you do know him and have seen him."

Jesus came into this world to show the way to God — to give a fuller revelation of God, so that men may approach Him. Jesus can do that because he is God in human flesh, who has life in himself while other forms of life depends on the Father who is the source of life.

Jesus' dialectic method of teaching evokes instant response but the poor grasp of the disciples contributes to what appears to be a comedy of errors: when he speaks spiritually they understand him materially. "Show us the Father and that is enough," says Philip, setting the stage for the next phase of the exposition. "Anyone who has seen me has seen the Father. I am in the Father and the Father is in me. The words I say to you are not just my own. Rather, it is the Father living in me, who is doing his work."

Jesus now presents the theme — the perfect dwelling place of God. It's man motivated and controlled by the Father of wisdom, knowledge and truth. Man is created to be the icon of His holiness and wisdom.

"Anyone who has faith in me will do what I have been doing, and even greater works than I do because I am going to the Father." The word `greater' must be understood as an extension of the work of Christ. Jesus never stepped out of Palestine and it was his disciples that carried his works to the greater parts of the world. And this verse should challenge every believer to great works.

And the believers' strength is answered prayer, which Jesus promises in these words: "I will do whatever you ask me in my name." Answered prayer is a promise to his disciples, who left everything, took up the cross and followed him. These disciples owned nothing and trusted the Lord to the uttermost. In other words, Jesus is assuring these men `You have not trusted me in vain.' Answered prayers are extended to genuine believers who surrender everything to the Lordship of Jesus and consider themselves as mere trustees of God's wealth, giving generously to the poor and for the extension of the kingdom of God. This brings glory to the Father as your works are the fruit of Jesus working in you even as the Father is working in and through the Son.

Now Jesus enters the next phase of the exposition — the Holy Spirit. He shows how the Holy Trinity works in the life of the believer. "If you love me, you will obey what I commanded. And I will ask the Father, and he will give you another Counsellor to be with you forever — the Spirit of Truth." It is a golden triangle of Love, Obedience and Power (read the Holy Spirit). Unless empowered by the Holy Spirit, a believer remains powerless, and useless.

Obedience is the key to a successful Christian enterprise: obedience to God's commandments in matters big and small and their ever striving to perfection. One can see the heart of God in Jesus when he says, "If you love me you will obey what I commanded." The King of Kings seeks to command obedience not out of fear but out of love, and he longs for your love because love is the character of God.

"The world cannot accept him (the Holy Spirit), because it neither sees him nor knows him. But you know him for he lives with you and will be in you." God's precious gifts are not for scoffers of the world but for the discerning who prize the things of God.

"I will not leave you as orphans; I will come to you. Before long, the world will not see me anymore, but you will see me. Because I live, you also will live." Jesus promises his disciples that his departure will not reduce them to the state of orphans. Because he will rise from the dead, they will live in him, by him, for him, and live the victorious life that conquered death and grave.

Much of what Jesus said then went above the heads of the disciples, but when they were empowered by the Holy Spirit on the day of Pentecost, they understood it all in flash back. "On that day you will realise that I am in the Father, and you are in me, and I am in you." Knowledge internalised is superior to abstract learning. And the realisation of `I in you' leads to the realisation of `You in me' which in turn leads to the realisation of `I am in the Father' which means the `Father in me'. It is an ascending experience to higher levels of awareness (read heaven). In other words, Christ's mission is to elevate human perception to divine scales.

"He who loves me will be loved by my Father, and I too will love him and show myself to him." The greatest privilege any human being can have is to be loved by the Father, his Maker and the God of time, space and eternity, who is also the everlasting spring of love, mercy and compassion.

That evening we hear Thomas, we hear Philip and we are about to hear Judas, not the traitor. But we hear less of Peter who must have been sobered by the warning that he would deny his Master three times that very night.

"But Lord, why do you intend to show yourself to us and not to the world?" Judas makes a point that unless the world comes to know who really Jesus is, how can he establish the kingdom of God. The mindset of the disciples is shaped by the idea of the Roman Empire and the Macedonian Empire but that the nature of the kingdom of God is something different they have yet to understand.

"All this I have spoken while still with you. But the

Counsellor, the Holy Spirit, who the Father will send in my name, will teach you all things and will remind you of everything I have told you."

The creative energy of God and the executing authority who moves men to do great things is the Third Person of the Trinity.

All things originate from the Father, is communicated through the Son and perfected by the Spirit. The Holy Spirit is called the Spirit of God because it proceeds from the Father, and also called the Spirit of Jesus because it is a gift of the Son and acts through him.

The effectiveness of a believer comes from the measure of the Holy Spirit in him, depending on the degree of his obedience to (the word of) God. The heroes of faith in the Old Testament and the New Testament were men empowered by the Spirit of God. By God's spirit, David braved lions and slew Goliath. By God's spirit, Solomon ruled wisely, the prophets foresaw events about to happen and Samson tamed the Philistines. By God's spirit, Peter cut the hearts of his audience, John soared into the theological firmament like an eagle that peers at the sun, Paul evangelized the Hellenistic world and wrote epistles, and the Apostles and martyrs laid down their lives for Christ.

The Holy Spirit is the great teacher who expounds scriptural truths to guide the honest believer to a meaningful life. The Spirit reminds the believer the things he has forgotten which Jesus has spoken, especially when he is about to err; and He dwells in his heart to be his invisible friend, philosopher and guide and an Ambassador of Jesus Christ.

By honouring the Father you honour the Son and the Holy Spirit, and by honouring the Son you honour the Father and the Holy Spirit, and by honouring the Holy Spirit you honour the Father and the Son. They are indivisible and of the same substance and nature, with one mind, one will, and one Spirit.

"Peace I leave with you; my peace I give you. I do not give to you as the world gives. Do not let your hearts be troubled and do not be afraid."

The exposition on troubled hearts ends in peace and joy, and ends the same way it began: "Let not your hearts be troubled." (The rhetoricians call it the circle technique). Peace and joy are the rewards of knowing the Living God. Peace with oneself flows from peace with God and leads to peace with others.

Haven't you noticed that some people carry their hell wherever they go? Because they don't have peace with themselves, they disturb everyone else's peace, even the harmony of society. Two illustrations will illumine the transforming power of Peace.

Paul and Silas, two evangelists of the early church, were lashed forty times by the Roman soldiers at Philippi for preaching Christ. Lacerated in the flesh, Paul and Silas were singing and rejoicing in the Lord, to the utter disbelief of the Philippian jailer, who was accustomed to seeing hardened criminals whining and cursing the whole night in a similar situation. Following an earthquake at night, the two were freed of their chains and the jailer was about to kill himself fearing the prized prisoners had escaped when he heard: "Do thyself no harm, we are here."

Trembling with fear, the jailer falls at their feet and asks, "What shall I do to be saved?" To which Paul and Silas replies, "Believe in the name of Lord Jesus, and you and your family will be saved." The jailer believes and is baptised. The peace and joy that God gives surpasses all understanding.

The next illustration is that of a king who went hunting and was thralled by the most melodious music he had ever heard. The king left the hunting expedition and pursued the heavenly voice and was shocked to find that it emanated from the flute of a leper without his nose and ears. Even a leper can enjoy the bliss of God's presence in his heart.

"I am going away... I have told you these things before so that when it happens you will believe. I will not speak to you much longer, for the prince of this world is coming. He has no hold on me, but the world must learn that I love the Father and I do exactly what the Father has commanded me. Come now, let's leave."

Jesus and his disciples are still in the Upper Room where the disciples are initiated into the deeper mystery of fellowship and life in the Spirit. As many as three times in the last six months he spoke of his impending death on the cross which is now just hours ahead. He foretold them to fortify their faith.

On another front, Satan the prince of this world who rules unrighteous hearts is advancing stealthily. In the purest and holiest life of Jesus, Satan could make no claim. In fact, the Son of God came to destroy the works of the devil, which is proliferation of wickedness on the planet, and to establish in its place the kingdom of God by the redeemed human race which is God's plan.

This time of the evening, the Kidron Brooke is red with the blood of the Passover lambs slain in Jerusalem. Jesus and his disciples are walking towards Mount Olives crossing the Kidron Valley. In the process, the true Passover Lamb dips his feet in the blood-red brook making redundant the shadow.

THE TRUE VINE

Vineyards sprawl on either side of the road to Mount Olives. Probably holding a vine in his hand, Jesus says, "I am the true vine, and my Father is the gardener. He cuts off every branch in me that bears no fruit, while every branch that does bear fruit he prunes so that it will be even more fruitful."

After the 4-fold mystery of 'I in you', 'You in me', 'I in the Father', and 'the Father in me', Jesus expounds the same truth — of abiding and fruit bearing — through another metaphor, the vine and the gardener. While some abide and bear fruit, many do not. The gardener deals with both; the fruitless he burns and the fruitful he prunes, painful that may be though. The message is terse: a good life bears abundant fruit but the wicked will be burned like the chaff.

"You are already clean because of the word I have spoken to you. Remain in me, and I will remain in you. No branch can bear fruit by itself; it must remain in the vine. Neither can you bear fruit unless you remain in me."

Because it proceeds from God, the Word has the power to cleanse — the power to edify and the power to make one wise. Wisdom leads to abiding, and abiding to fruit bearing. And sanctification by the word is a precondition for bearing fruit.

From the imagery of the vine and the gardener the focus now shifts to the vine and the branches. "I am the vine; you are the branches. If a man remains in me and I in him, he will bear much fruit; apart from me you can do nothing..."

Religious fanatics kill a young missionary in Old Delhi, and his sister comes from England and starts a college to educate members of the rabid community; and that enterprise becomes St Stephen's college. A lady witnesses the tragedy of a poor woman dying during childbirth, unattended by a doctor or a midwife. This lady goes back to her home country, raises funds and starts a hospital in the very place, which is the famous Vellore Hospital in Chennai. A young Priest is moved by the plight of lepers that he volunteers to go to serve in an island of lepers and becomes the renowned Father Damien. The story of Florence Nightingale is yet another that merits mention.

History is replete with examples of the saga of courage and sacrifice men and women who abided in the vine have displayed, bearing abundant fruit. The branches and the vine have an organic — not organisational — relationship which cannot be severed without damage to the branches.

"If you remain in me and my words in you, ask whatever you wish and it will be given you. This is to my Father's glory that you bear much fruit, showing yourselves to be my disciples." To remain in Christ means to let the Word dwell in you richly, controlling your life, your decisions and desires.

The Word leads to holy living, so your desires and prayers become godly — the very things God wants in your life. When two persons have the same mind and the same spirit, they are said to walk together; and when you have the same mind and spirit of God, you walk with God, and your Seventh Sense gets activated to listen to the voice of God. Then your prayers are answered because they are an extension of God's vision, wisdom and plan for your life.

Bearing abundant fruit by living in Christ brings glory to the Father. And life is an opportunity to do great things for God and all great things start with the single step of trusting Him. Every good deed that you do and every accomplishment that you make honours your Father in heaven.

Jesus now introduces the greatest theme of all. "As the Father has loved me, so have I loved you. Now remain in my love. If you obey my commandments, you will remain in my love. Just as I have obeyed my Father's commandment and remain in his care."

Do you hear the heartbeat of Christ longing for your love? The human race is specially designed to love God. Love proceeds from the heart of God and all who respond realise the infinite joy that comes from God.

Love is not a fleeting emotion but a deep commitment to doing the will of the loved one, and love of God is a deeper commitment to doing the will of God reflected in His commandments. Obedience is the unmistakable proof of a living relationship with God that cannot be broken by external forces.

"I have told you this so that my joy may be in you and that your joy may be complete."

The goal of life is to know God and to enjoy Him evermore. God lives in a state of eternal bliss and knowing Him is experiencing a foretaste of heaven. Jesus says in the Book of Revelation, "I knock at the door and if anyone opens the door, I will come in and sup with him." Communing with God has its infinite rewards of joy.

"My command is this: Love each other as I have loved you. Greater love has no one than this, that he lay down his life for his friends."

Love is not taking, grabbing and acquiring but giving, surrendering and sacrificing. The greatest sacrifice one could offer is to give one's own life. Jesus is pouring out his life as a libation. His sacrificial love should bind the disciples into a close-knit brotherhood; and set a golden chain of love through centuries till He returns – embracing every nation, culture and geographic entity.

"You are my friends if you do what I command. I no longer call you servants because a servant does not know his master's business. Instead, I have called you friends, for everything that I learned from my Father, I have made known to you."

What a privilege for mortals to be the friend of the immortal one! The Son of God came to reveal the Father in full measure so that through the Son you have full access to God.

"You did not choose me, but I chose you and appointed you to go and bear fruit — fruit that will last. Then the Father will give you whatever you ask in my name. This is my command: Love each other."

The disciples are chosen to bear fruit, abundant fruit; and fruit is faith in action and abundant fruit abundant faith in action. Prayer in Jesus' name has power because he grants his disciples the power to act on his behalf. Every fruit-bearing believer has appropriated this power to the Father's glory.

THE WORLD HATES YOU

"If the world hates you, keep in mind that it hated me first. If you belonged to the world, it would love you as its own. As it is you do not belong to the world, but I have chosen you out of the world. That is why the world hates you."

The 'world' here denotes a godless system directly controlled by Satan who opposes truth, holiness and righteousness. Satan hates truth because he is a liar and the father of lies; he hates holiness because it is contrary to his character; and he hates righteousness because he is the antithesis of it. Nevertheless he seeks to be worshipped in place of God and strives to be the centre of all cosmic activity.

Satan is a spiritual being with superhuman intelligence, superhuman power and superhuman will. He works by deception and plays on the emotions, foibles and weaknesses of people to turn them away from the Living God by supplying fake gods. He delights in false worship and proliferation of wickedness. God has granted free will to all created beings to know and worship Him in their freedom. To Satan and his rebellious evil spirits, God has designed a place that serves them right.

In a world that hates and persecutes the righteous, Jesus has called the disciples to be his shining witnesses – shining in the dark wicked world.

"Remember the words I spoke to you: No servant is greater than his master. If they persecuted me, they will persecute you also. If they obeyed my teaching, they will obey yours also. They will treat you this way because of my name, for they do not know the One who sent me."

Genuine disciples cannot escape persecution in a God-hating world. The world detests them because it has not known God, the source of Life.

"If I had not come and spoken to them, they would not be guilty of sin. Now, however, they have no excuse for their sin. He who hates me hates my Father as well. If I had not done among them what no one else did, they would not be guilty of sin. But now they have seen the miracles, and yet they have hated both me and my Father. But this is to fulfil what is written in their Law: They hated me without reason."

A stubborn refusal to accept the truth that God reveals is sin of the worst kind. The Jewish leaders who have both heard him and seen his miracles belong to this blighted category. They are only fulfilling the prophesy of Isaiah, foretold some six hundred years ago that they would hate him without reason. The only reason for hate is sin in the heart.

"When the Counsellor comes, whom I will send you from the Father, the Spirit of truth who goes out from the Father, he will testify about me. And you also must testify, for you have been with me from the beginning."

The Holy Spirit — the third person of the Trinity and the Spirit of Truth who proceeds from the Father of Truths whom Jesus will send after his ascension to heaven — will witness to the deity of Jesus, even as the disciples will proclaim it across the world.

"All this I have told you so that you will not go astray. They will put you out of the synagogue; in fact, a time is coming when anyone who kills you will think he is offering a service to God."

Christ warns them of impending persecution and prepares them to face it with divine courage and divine dignity. Persecution, no doubt, will begin at home with the synagogues and later with imperial Rome and the nations of the world that feel threatened by the spread of the gospel. Nevertheless, it is persecution that has fanned the growth of faith.

And some people are so fanatic that they deem killing the righteous a religious act.

"They will do such things because they have not known the Father or me. I have told you this, so that when the time comes you will remember that I warned you, I did not tell you this at first because I was with you."

If religion does not take us to the Living God, it is a sad commentary on religion: this life is a nursery for something better to come — an after-life of greater awareness, greater happiness, greater purposefulness. Those who lead a wanton life here are in for a jolt at the day of reckoning. "Do not be afraid of people who can kill you, but be afraid of someone who can cast where the flame never dies," Jesus had taught the disciples on an earlier occasion.

THE COUNSELLOR GOD

"Now I am going to him who sent me, yet none of you asks me, `Where are you going?' Because I have said these things, you are filled with grief. But I tell you the truth: It is for your good that I am going away. Unless I go away, the Counsellor will not come to you. But if I go, I will send him to you."

The grief-stricken disciples were so benumbed to ask him, 'Lord, where are you going?' But he assures them it is profitable that he goes to the Father because then they will receive the Holy Spirit to guide them through the rough and tumble of their life, which is the principal benefit of his impending sacrifice on Calvary. The Holy Spirit will energise them as if by a superior electricity equipping them for divine works.

"When he comes, he will convict the world of guilt in regard to sin, and righteousness and judgement: in regard to sin, because some do not believe in me; in regard to righteousness, because I am going to the Father, where you can see me no longer; and in regard to judgement, because the prince of this world now stands condemned."

Creating an awareness of one's own moral depravity and preparing a climate for repentance is the first phase of the Ministry of the Holy Spirit in a person's life. The person then looks to Calvary for the blood cleansing and seeks God's righteousness given free. This is the heart of the gospel that God so loved humanity that He gave His only begotten son that whoever believes in him shall not perish but have eternal life. God's standards of righteousness are too high for human effort to achieve. But if you reject God's love and the life-transforming ministry of the Holy Spirit, you stand condemned. But already condemned are Satan and his evil spirits because of what they are.

"I have much more to say to you, more than you can now bear. But when he, the Spirit of truth, comes, he will guide you into all truth. He will not speak on his own; he will speak only what he hears, and he will tell you what is yet to come. He will bring glory to me by taking from what is mine and making it known to you. All that belongs to the Father is mine. That is why I said the Spirit will take from what is mine and make it known to you."

To enumerate for easy understanding, the first ministry of the Holy Spirit is to **convict**, the second ministry is to **teach** the believers the deeper truths of Salvation and guide them towards perfection. The third ministry is to equip the evangelists to **preach** the Gospel. The fourth ministry is **foretelling and forth-telling** of events, which the prophets and apostles did. Foretelling is prophesying so that believers are warned of the dangers ahead and events to come; and forth-telling is speaking out against unrighteous living. The fifth ministry is **glorifying Christ and illumining the Word of God**. The sixth ministry is **unifying** the believer in the Holy Trinity and thereby glorifying the Father. All that belongs to the Father belongs to the Son and all that belongs to the Son belongs to the Holy Spirit, and all that belongs to the Spirit is shared by the believers in the perfect unity of heaven.

"In a little while you will see me no more, and then after a little while you will see me." Jesus now tells his disciples they will miss him for a while but meet him again in his glorified body after his resurrection.

And a third time Jesus assures the disciples, "Until now you have not asked for anything in my name. Ask and you will receive, and your joy will be complete." The proof of his deity and resurrection is answered prayer, promised to the believer for his joy and confidence in the Lord.

THE HIGH PRIESTLY PRAYER

"After this, he looked heavenward and prayed: Father, the time has come. Glorify your Son that your Son may glorify you. For you granted him authority over all people that he might give eternal life to all those whom you have given him. Now this is eternal life: that they may know you, the only true God, and Jesus Christ, whom you have sent."

Christ's mission on earth is to reveal the living God and impart a deeper experience of Him, which is eternal life. The Son existed even before the foundation of the universe and shared the same glory of the Father. Now he is returning to his Father to share the same glory and to be seated at His right hand. And the time has come to reveal himself as the God of Life who conquered death. Remember, he had once told his mother at Cana during the wedding feast, 'My time has not come'; and he had told his brothers who wanted him to go to the feast in Jerusalem, `My time has not come'; and he had told the Jewry at Jerusalem during an encounter, `My time has not come.' Now clearly his time has come.

"I have brought you glory on earth by completing the work you have given me to do. And now, Father, glorify me in your presence with the glory I had with you before the world began."

Glory is the divine essence and in application it means revealing the character and presence of God, which is what Christ did every moment of his life on earth. He is now heaven-bound, returning to his Father's glory.

Book Six

"I have revealed you to those whom you gave me out of the world. Now they know that everything you have given me comes from you. For I gave them the words you gave me and they accepted them. They knew with certainty that I came from you, and they believed that you sent me. I pray for them."

Jesus prays for his disciples who have the word of truth and know that every good thing comes from the Father. How can God deal with anyone who does not believe that He exists — except as a judge? Scripture points out our sin, and motivates us to confess and renew our relationship with God; it is the mariner's compass guiding us to the truth.

"I am not praying for the world, but for those you have given me, for they are yours. All I have is yours and you have is mine. And glory has come to me through them. I will remain in the world no longer, but they are still in the world, and I am coming to you. Holy Father, protect them by the power of your name — the name you gave me — so that they may be one as we are one. While I was with them, I protected them and kept them safe by that name you gave me. None has been lost except the son of perdition so that scripture would be fulfilled."

His concern as he is leaving them is two fold: their protection from the evil one, and their unity in the Spirit. He places them before the Father saying he protected them as long as he was in the world in His name except Judas the son of perdition — who is not programmed to destruction but chose his own destruction as scripture prophesies.

"I am coming to you now, but I say these things while I am still in the world, so that they may have the full measure of my joy within them. I have given them your word and the world has hated them, for they are not of the world any more than I am of the world."

The farewell is not an occasion to mourn but to fill the cup of joy that springs from holiness and he prays that this joy may remain with the disciples even after his departure. The Word is the key to the joy that he leaves behind in a world that hates them.

"My prayer is not that you take them out of the world but that you protect them from the evil one. They are not of the world even as I am not of the world. Sanctify them by the truth; your word is truth. As you sent me into the world, I have sent them into the world. For them I sanctify myself, that they too may be sanctified truly."

The crafty fox Satan has wicked designs to thwart God's kingdom. As soon as infant Jesus is born in a manger, Satan plays on the jealousy of Herod to kill the child; in the wilderness he tempts Jesus with spurious means to establish the kingdom of God which is rejected outright; then he provokes the Jewry to stone Christ to death at least twice but Jesus escapes each time; and he gets ready for a final confrontation at Calvary and before that at Gethsemane but Satan will be beaten and vanquished. So he will turn his attention to the disciples. Therefore Jesus trains them in holiness through the word and equips them for the task ahead. He who needs no sanctification formally sanctifies himself for their sake. Sanctification lends effectiveness in preaching the kingdom and is a counter-offensive to Satan's strategy.

"My prayer is not for them alone. I pray also for those who will believe in me through their message, that all of them may be one, Father, just as you are in me and I am in you. May they also be in us so that the world may believe that you have sent me. I have given them the glory that you gave me, that they may be one as we are one: I in you and you in me. May they be brought to complete unity to let the world know that you sent me and have loved them even as you have loved me."

Jesus' high priestly prayer extends to all believers — you and me who have put our trust in Christ through the words of the disciples coming down to our generation to produce a grand unity of believers in holiness. This unity in holiness is the proof that God sent his Son into the world and that the Father loves all those who trust the Son and shares his indwelling glory even as the Father shares his glory with the Son. The good news is that you and me are in the mind of God, no matter what the world thinks of us.

"Father, I want those you have given me to be with me where I am, and to see my glory, the glory you have given me because you loved me before the creation of the world."

Jesus wants his disciples to behold and share his glory, the glory that he left behind to be born in a manger in the lowliest fashion so that he may lift up the lowliest to celestial glory.

"Righteous Father, though the world does not know you, I know you, and they know that you have sent me. I have made you known to them, and will continue to make you known in order that the love you have for me may be in them and that I myself may be in them."

Christ's high priestly prayer ends on a unique note, radiating the Father's infinite love. And Christ invites all humanity to share the Father's love. A prayer springing from the depth of love will surely touch the heart of God and that is the secret of answered prayers.

(Read the rest of the book with a meditating heart; if you will the truth of God will touch your heart).

THE LONGEST NIGHT

It was the night of betrayal, arrest and desertion. It was the night when human frailties enacted a drama of cowardice. It was the night when the forces of darkness tried to snuff out the divine spark. His disciples fled in panic, one of them turned a traitor to betray, the temple guards and Roman soldiers lay hands on him, all in quick succession. But it was not yet.

Jesus and his disciples were already in Gethsemane. For Jesus it was prayer time, and every situation in life he faced with prayer. Prayer is not a sign of weakness or a substitute for action. In fact, prayer strengthens action, sharpens the mind, and illumines the road ahead. Prayer is communion with the Father who blesses, who guides and who empowers.

You will never understand the agony that Jesus faced at Gethsemane. The next day, he would face the outpouring of God's wrath for the sins of the world — the sins of the first man to the sins of the last man on earth — so that humanity is spared of God's righteous wrath. God is absolute holiness and righteousness and any sin is an affront to His holiness and righteousness. God demands justice, the just punishment for every sin committed by every human being. But God is also absolute mercy and absolute love, and in His mercy and love, God has sent his Son to take upon himself this punishment on behalf of humanity. This is called God's plan of salvation. Since the guilty cannot be punished twice for the same offence, those who acknowledge the atoning sacrifice at Calvary are spared. On the Day of Judgement, you either stand before God as your judge or as your Father depending on whether or not you have accepted the grace of the gospel, which is free forgiveness. What the Son of God will accomplish at the cross is termed redemption, which is for all humanity. It is not a license to sin but a way to holiness.

Jesus asks the disciples to "keep awake and pray," something they find so difficult at that hour. "My soul is exceedingly sorrowful unto death," he tells them. It was the second watch of night when the simple folks would retire to bed after a weary day's toil. Slumber and sorrow made their eyelids heavy and they did what was most natural at night.

Jesus took the trio, Peter, James and John, his soul mates in the hour of agony, a few yards away and asked them to keep awake and pray. Jesus himself went ahead a stone-throwaway, knelt down and prayed: "Father, if it is possible, take this cup away from me, because all things are possible for you; nevertheless, be it as you wish, not as I wish." That moment, Jesus came very close to the frailties of the flesh and blood; but the next moment, his divinity expressed itself.

On the cross tomorrow, he who knew no sin would be carrying the burden of the most repulsive thing for the deity, the (imputed) sin of the world; and hence he would be cut off from the Father's communion that was ever his delight. The very thought turned his sweat into thick drops of blood. Jesus was pre-living the morrow in his Father's presence to gain strength.

When Jesus returned to his disciples it was as if they were engaged in a sleeping contest, each vying with the other to score snoring aces. Jesus had been praying for an hour or so but that seemed too long even for Peter, James and John to keep awake. He gently wakes them up nevertheless and asks them to keep praying, lest they should enter into temptation.

"The spirit is indeed willing but the flesh is weak," he reminded them and again went ahead and prayed. A second time he returned to find them peacefully sleeping, blissfully unaware of the agony of the Son of Man. He did not disturb them but went and prayed a third time and returned only to find them in deep sleep. This time he woke them up to witness what was to happen for which they were chosen.

"..Behold the hour is at hand and the Son of Man is being betrayed into the hands of sinners. Rise, let us be going. See my betrayer is at hand."

Even as he was speaking, a great multitude appeared with clubs and swords and lantern. Leading them was Judas with a beaming smile and outstretched arms ready to embrace his Master. Duplicity unadulterated masked the man Judas who was under the total control of the prince of duplicity, Satan.

The traitor advanced and planted two kisses on the cheeks of Jesus, long enough to be identified by the captors in waiting so that they don't catch one of the 12 and march away in false triumph.

Roman soldiers wielding swords and temple guards carrying clubs closed in as if encountering a gang of robbers. The Jewry have procured a Roman garrison and Roman garrisons were stationed in Jerusalem during the festival season to prevent any outbreak of riots, something the ruling class always feared. An estimated crowd of 600 descended on the 12, five against each one of the Galileans.

Judas's exuding affection and prolonged kiss deceived none but himself.

"Friend, why have you come? You betray the Son of Man with a kiss?"

Now Judas recedes into the background, having done his signalling job and unwittingly accomplishing God's own plan.

"What do you seek?" Jesus asks the crowd.

"Jesus of Nazareth," they said.

"I am he," he said.

The crowd that sought to arrest him fell backwards. Again he asked,

"Whom do you seek?"

"Jesus of Nazareth."

"I am he."

The crowd tried to surge ahead, but again fell backwards. A third time he asked,

"Whom do you seek?"

"Jesus of Nazareth"

"I am he."

The crowd fell backwards a third time as if a magnetic field is active around the person of Jesus. But that the scriptures might be fulfilled he gave himself up.

Peter gave a live demonstration of his raw courage; brandishing the sword he cut off the ear of the high priest's servant, missing his neck narrowly. Obviously, Simon wasn't aiming at his ear, but the fisherman lacked the skill of a sword's man to hit the bull's eye. Instantly, Jesus restores the ear and admonishes Peter,

"He who takes the sword shall fall by it."

"Put your sword into the sheath. Shall I not drink the cup which my Father has given me?"

And Jesus turned to the mob and said, "You have come against me as a robber, with swords and clubs. I was in your temple daily but you did not seize me. But this is your hour and the power of darkness."

Then the mob seized Jesus and the disciples fled finding that he does nothing to save himself. A young lad stood nearby, taken aback by the scene. Clearly he was not amused and the mob caught hold of him but he fled naked, leaving the outer garments in the hand of the captors. The lad, presumably John Mark the writer of the second gospel, followed the mob that first swooped in on the Upper Room thinking Jesus and his disciples were still there. Finding that they had already left, the mob came to the garden of Gethsemane where there was an olive press. Alarmed by the spectacle John Mark hurried along wrapping himself up in his outer garment. What happened to John Mark would have happened to the disciples had they stayed on — they would have been caught, beaten and tried along with Jesus if not crucified.

They bound him and led him to the house of Annas, who was the former high priest and the father-in-law of Caiphas the high priest and the real power behind the throne. Peter and John followed the mob and the younger secured the elder admission into the courtyard of Annas' since John knew the family presumably through Zebedi's trade. Trouble was lurking for Peter as the servant girl who kept the door said, "You are one of this man's disciples, are you?"

"O, no, I am not," Simon replied before he knew what he said. A little later, Simon saw some servants and officers making a fire of coal to warm themselves in the cold. He found the fire too tempting and moved towards it unmindful of the company. Annas the old fox was questioning Jesus on his doctrine and disciples, to which Jesus said, "I spoke openly and ask those who heard me."

According to the Jewish practice, the accused is never cross-examined but the witnesses, and if they agree, the guilt is established. Jesus is pointing to the impropriety of the high priestly conducts.

To gain favour, one of the high priest's henchmen struck Jesus and said, "Do you answer the high priest like this!"

"Bear witness, if I have spoken falsehood; if I spoke the truth, why strike me?"

Meekness is not silence, nor silence righteousness, faced with injustice.

The trial then shifted to the house of Caiphas in the adjacent compound with Jesus bound and led. Peter was seen in the same company warming himself. "Surely, you are one of them; you are a Galilean, your accent shows it," said they who stood by. "Surely, I don't know the man," Simon began to protest and swear and curse.

A little later, a relative of the high priest's servant whose ear Peter cut off said, 'Did I not see you in the garden with him?' A third time Simon denied vehemently, and the rooster crowed a second time. The Lord turned and looked at Simon, and Simon broke down and wept bitterly, going out of the precincts of the high priestly mansion. Those eyes of love and compassion seemed more eloquent than all the sermons he had heard. Simon knew he breached the confidence of his Master for the high calling. Biographers write that it became a habit with the Great Fisherman to rise up early with the rooster and stand on his knees to weep every morning the rest of his life that furrows of tears could be seen on his cheeks.

Now the chief priests, elders and members of the Supreme Jewish Council sought to find false testimony against Jesus in order to execute him — for which, of course, they needed the Roman Governor's approval. Testimony after testimony collapsed and finally someone came forward and said they heard him say, "I am able to destroy the temple of God and to build it in three days."

Seemingly satisfied, the high priest Caiphas asked, "What is it that these people are saying against you?"

Jesus did not open his mouth as the trial was fabricated. The chief priest then changed his strategy:

"I put you under oath by the living God: Tell us if you are the Christ, the Son of God?"

It was time for Jesus to speak in the name of God. "It is as you said. Nevertheless, I say to you, hereafter you will see the Son of Man sitting at the right hand of God, and coming on the clouds of heaven."

"Blasphemy," said the chief priest and tore his clothes. "Why do we need witnesses now. You have heard it yourself. What do you think?"

"He deserves death," they concluded.

Then they spat on him, blindfolded him, struck him, mocked him and asked him, 'Prophesy, Christ, who struck you?' When they had finished with the cruel sport, early in the morning they led him to the Roman governor's residence, the Pretorium, to be condemned to death.

JUDGEMENT

Pilate hated the Jews to the hilt, especially their hypocrisy and pretension to a superior race. He loved to teach the Jews a lesson and he thought the sooner he did the better. But Caesar stood like a Colossus before every Roman official, and to Caesar he looked for his promotions and prosperity. Caesar could launch a thousand careers and wreck a ten thousand. By Caesar young officers rose, took influential brides and walked into the inner circle of Rome. True, it was Alexander the Great who first conquered the whole of the civilised world, but it was the Romans who invented a durable system of government to rule the world. And the Romans needed the power-hungry natives like the Herods, the Annas and the Caiaphas to perpetuate their rule, as much as the Herods, the Annas and the Caiaphas needed Rome to strengthen their position. No doubt in politics those who hate each other sometimes make good partners for reasons of the state. Hence the dictum, the state before self, the catch-word of every hypocrite.

If Pilate wanted to teach the Jews a lesson, that fatal Friday was not the one for it. At dawn, he was abruptly woken up from his bed by a Jewish commotion right at the gate of the Pretorium. They brought a man who they said was a rabble-rouser and a troublemaker who dissuaded people from paying taxes to Caesar because he himself claimed he was the king of the Jews. Bad day, thought Pilate preparing to make his public appearance; but it proved to be the worst day of his life.

One look at the man convinced Pilate that he was not from

the ordinary folk. His supreme sangfroid and serenity made a deep impression on the Roman governor. The man looked like one of those Greek philosophers who had come to give a discourse rather than a malefactor or a criminal. Pilate could not take his eyes off the man as he saw a spark of divinity in his eyes.

"Are you the king of the Jews?" Pilate enquired.

"You say it already," Jesus replied.

Pilate wanted to avoid a miscarriage of justice because he knew it was the jealousy of the Jewry that drove it to this insane act.

They began to testify against him and accuse him but his icy calm and his chilling silence astounded Pilate.

"What have you to say, your own nation and chief priests have delivered you into my hands?"

"My kingdom is not of this world. If it were, my servants would fight to prevent my arrest. But my kingdom is from another place. I came to bear witness to the truth."

"You are a King, then!"

"You are right in saying I am a King. In fact, for this reason I was born, and for this I came into the world, to testify to the truth. Everyone on the side of truth listens to me."

"What is truth?" asked Pilate but would not wait for a reply. He walked to the Jewry to declare, "This man is innocent and I found no guilt in him."

On every Jewish festival, the Roman governor would release a Jewish prisoner and this time Pilate suggested he would release Jesus.

"We want Barabas, we want Barabas. Away with this man," the crowd shouted. "He stirs up the people all the way from Galilee to this place."

When Pilate heard he was a Galilean under Herod's jurisdiction, he decided to send him to Herod who was also in town for the festival. The governor thought that way he could escape the ordeal of trial.

Pilate's gesture pleased Herod, who was willing to forget all the snubs the governor had so far meted out to him. He was more than delighted to see the Galilean hoping he would perform some miracles in the court. But the Galilean paid little attention to Herod. The chief priests and elders brought a volley of charges, but Jesus met them by an admonishing silence.

Then the court mocked the Galilean and the soldiers arrayed him in gorgeous rob befetting a King and placed a crown on his head and sceptre in his hand. But they were careful not to tread on the sentiments of their fellow Galileans, who sought him the most.

To the unwilling Pilate, Jesus was returned and the trial resumed. On the judgement seat sat Pilate a second time when a messenger from his wife arrived with a warning, "Have nothing to do with that righteous man, I suffered terrible things in my dream because of him." Pilate was startled by the conspiracy of circumstances that zeroed in one him.

A second time he pleaded with the Jewry hoping to persuade them but in vain.

"Whom should I release, Barabas or your King?"

"We want Barabas, we want Barabas, we want Barabas."

"Then what shall I do with your King?"

"Crucify him, crucify him, crucify him. We have no king but Caesar."

Pilate thought he would scourge the man to appease the mob. So the ruthless Roman soldiers executed it to perfection — with a whip that splits the victims back, not once but forty times minus one, and the tiny pieces of iron and the small bone at the tip of the whip furrowing the flesh.

The soldiers twisted together a crown of thorns and put it on his head. They clothed him in a purple robe and went up to him saying, "Hail King of the Jews." They struck him in the face and repeatedly on the head as brutally as they had made a pulp of his back. Even hardened criminals collapsed and normally the victims were half-dead by the end of the scourging.

"Behold the man," Pilate told the Jewry hoping this cruel sport would satiate their blood-thirst.

For the last time Pilate asked the mob, "Should I release him or Barabas?"

As soon as the chief priests and elders saw Jesus with the crown of thorns and purple robe, they cried all the more "Crucify him, crucify him, crucify him."

"Why? What crime has this man committed?"

"We have a law, and according to it he must die, because he claimed to be the Son of God."

When Pilate heard this, he was even more afraid — He summoned Jesus inside the Palace and asked, "Where do you come from?"

Jesus gave him no reply. Did he who asked him what is truth but would not wait for a reply deserve a reply?

An amazed Pilate asked him, "You refuse to speak to me? Don't you realise I have power either to free you or to crucify you?"

"You would have no power over me if it were not given to you from above. Therefore, the one who handed me over to you is guilty of a greater sin." Jesus was reminding Pilate of the consequences of human actions. And Pilate sought all the more to release Jesus.

"If you release him you are not a friend of Caesar."

Pilate shuddered at the very mention of Caesar. He knew he lost the game. Should someone go and whisper in Caesar's ear... that thought was spine-chilling. The bloodhounds were still hungry and would be satisfied with nothing less than this innocent man on the cross, whoever he may be.

Pilate sat on the judgement seat a third time, to make a mockery of justice. Imagine, the federal judge declares, "The grand jury finds this man innocent but we send him to the gallows!"

Exasperated, exhausted and fatigued, Pilate thought of his wife's warning. A thousand voices rang simultaneously in his ear, "Keep away from the blood of that righteous man." Who really is this man, Pilate wondered.

Torn between the fear of nemeses and the fear of Caesar, Pilate surrendered to Caesar and postponed nemeses because Caesar is the present tense and nemeses the future tense.

A visibly shaken and nervous Pilate took water in front of the mob and washed his hands of the guilt.

"I am innocent of this man's blood," pronounced the governor.

"Let his blood be upon us and our children," the wildly excited mob shouted, knowing little what consequences it would bring upon their children and children's children.

Pilate passed the judgement and passed into history as the man who sentenced Christ to the cross. That is the only reason the world remembers him today.

Judas of Kiriotha found that his plans had gone awry as Jesus was condemned to die. He always thought his Master would escape either to proclaim himself King or to go on with his teaching and healing ministry till the appointed time. Now he stood exposed as a traitor, a downright villainous traitor.

"I betrayed innocent blood," he exploded into remorse and could not forgive himself. He ran to the chief priests and burst out but they were unmoved. In utter despair he threw those silver pieces, the betrayal money, into the temple and hanged himself on a tree.

Book Seven

THE KING OF THE JEWS

If the trial of Christ was a mockery of justice, his execution was a panic reaction of those who were afraid of the truth. Between 6 and 7 am he stood on trial before Pilate and around 9 am he was on the cross at Golgotha better known as Calvary. Why did the Jewry act in such indecent haste when the prevalent Roman laws granted at least two days for the condemned to be with the family and friends? Probably the Jewry was afraid of an uprising of the mob or his escape through supernatural powers. Even Judas who betrayed never expected any harm coming to him because he had seen him escape at least two times through the crowd when the Jewry took stones to kill him. Nevertheless, it was in God's plan that he must shed his righteous blood for the redemption of humanity, and he had come not to escape but fulfil it.

Moved by the Holy Spirit Prophet Isaiah wrote some 700 years before Christ was born:

> Surely, he took up our infirmities
> and carried our sorrows,
> yet we consider him stricken by God,
> smitten by him, and afflicted.
> But he was pierced for our transgressions,
> **he was crushed for our iniquities;**
> the punishment that brought us peace was upon him,
> and by his wounds we are healed.

We all, like sheep, have gone astray,
each of us has turned to his own way;
and the Lord has laid on him
the iniquity of us all.
He was oppressed and afflicted,
yet he did not open his mouth;
he was led like a lamb to the slaughter,
and as a sheep before her shearers is silent,
so he did not open his mouth.
By oppression and judgment he was taken away.
And who can speak of his descendants?
For he was cut off from the land of the living;
for the transgression of my people, he was stricken.
He was assigned a grave with the wicked,
and with the rich in his death,
though he had done no violence,
nor was any deceit in his mouth.
Yet it was the Lord's will to crush him and
cause him to suffer,
and though the Lord makes his life a guilt offering...

A beautiful illustration in the Book of Genesis prefigures the atoning sacrifice of Christ. God appears to Abraham in a vision to test his faith and asks him to sacrifice his only son, the son of his long wait of a quarter of a century. On the third day of his journey with his son and servants, he reaches Mount Moria, now Mount Calvary. Leaving behind his servants, Abraham and his son Isaac climb the mount with the latter carrying the wood and fire for the sacrifice.

Noticing something was amiss, Isaac asks his father, "Father, where is the lamb for the burnt offering?"

"God himself will provide the lamb, my son," replied Abraham in earnest faith.

Abraham builds an altar, arranges the wood, binds his son and lays him on the wood atop the altar. Then he took the knife to slay his son, but the angel of the Lord called out to him, "Abraham, Abraham!"

"Here I am."

"Do not lay a hand on the boy. Do not do anything to him. Now I know that you fear God, because you have not withheld from me your son, your only son."

Abraham looked up and saw in the bush a ram caught up by its horns. He took the ram and offered it as a burnt offering, instead of his son.

Christ is the Lamb of God, the only one who ever lived without sin, whose purest blood has the power to redeem mankind.

As for Abraham, he believed God is the God of life and death, and should he sacrifice his son God can bring him back to life the next moment. In effect, Abraham believed in resurrection and earned the epithet the Father of the Faithful.

If it was God's plan that Christ must suffer and die on the cross, puny little humans can only facilitate it: of course, out of their own free will.

So the hammer, the nails, the cross, food for soldiers, all were made ready in haste. Four soldiers would guard each cross under a centurion. The condemned would carry the cross to the site of execution, sometimes hands tied to it with cords. Led by the centurion, the procession normally took the longest route and the most crowded streets — a white board in front proclaiming the offence of the guilty to be executed. That fatal Friday the longest route was abandoned for the haste of the Jewry to see Jesus on the cross.

The cross is the cruelest and most painful form of execution. A Phoenician invention adapted by the Romans as exemplary punishment for crimes against the state, like treason and rioting. The cross in those days had three patterns: St Andrew's cross in the shape of letter 'X', the cross in the form of letter 'T' and the Latin cross in the shape of symbol plus (+). And Christ was crucified on a Latin cross. The cross was almost unheard of before the time of the Caesars.

From the Palace of Herod where once stood the Palace of King David, started the melancholic procession. Descending to the gate of the First Wall, it passed through the busy quarter of Acra where the shops were closed for the Passover. Men lined up the street and women stopped their festive preparations, came out and raised loud lamentations. He neither ate nor drank nor slept since the Last Supper — going through the agony at Gethsemane, betrayal in the garden and the trials in succession by Annas, Caiphas, Pilate, Herod, and again Pilate. He was moving from indignity to torture. All in one night and the dawn. His pallid face bore bloodstains from the crown of thorns. And his mangled body could no more bear the burden on his shoulders.

When the procession reached the City Gate came a man from across — a man named Simon from the Jewish colony in Cyrene on the outskirts of Jerusalem. The soldiers commanded him to do the job he was not especially delighted to do. Little did Simon know by that one act he was entering the twilight of fame. The cross still on Jesus' shoulders, Simon carried the major weight supporting it from behind.

Precisely when the procession halted for Simon to carry the beam, the women of Jerusalem closed in and wept. While entering Jerusalem, Jesus wept, and the women wept as he was leaving the city.

"Daughters of Jerusalem, do not weep for me; weep for yourselves and your children. For the time will come when you say, `Blessed are the barren women, and the wombs that never bore, and the breasts that never nursed!' Then `they will say to the mountains, Fall on us! and to the hills, Cover us!' "

In less than forty years hence, nemesis would visit the city that crucified their King, and hundreds of crosses would rise till there was not sufficient room or wood. Jewish historian Josephus records that a frenzied mother roasted her own child and in the mockery of desperation reserved half of that horrible meal for those murderers who daily broke in upon her to rob her of what scanty food had been left her. In those days of tribulation, how often women longed for childlessness and desired the quick death by falling mountain rocks hillsides rather than prolonged torture.

Around nine o'clock, the procession ended at Golgotha, and the execution started step by step. First, the upright wood was planted in the ground, and the feet of the crucified normally two feet above the ground. Then the transverse wood was placed on the ground, and the condemned laid on it, arms extended, drawn up and bound to it. And a strong, sharp nail was driven, first into the right hand and then into the left. The condemned was drawn up by means of ropes, sometimes with the help of ladders; the transverse was either bound or nailed to the upright, and a support for the body fastened on it. Lastly, the feet was extended and either one nail hammered into each or a larger piece of iron through the two. The victim hangs for two days or three, even a week, in unutterable anguish. Breathing becomes difficult as hours pass by since he has to lift his body up each time against its sinking weight. The breathing grows heavier and heavier till the body is unable to lift itself, and he swoons and death follows.

It was a Jewish practice to serve a cocktail of strong wine mixed with myrrh to deaden the consciousness of the hapless led to the execution. It was an act of charity whose cost is born by the women of Jerusalem. Having tasted it, Jesus would drink it no more because he would like to meet death in full consciousness.

In Latin, Greek and Aramaic, the title on the cross proclaimed, **Jesus of Nazareth King of the Jews**. Smarting under the jesting slight of Pilate, the Jewish authorities rushed back to the governor. Somebody might have noticed the title while Jesus was being led to Golgotha and reported to the Jewry. The Jews won't enter the court of the Roman governor, because they would become unholy dealing with a non-Jew at such close quarters, thus disqualifying them from eating the Passover feast.

"What I have written, I have written," growled the governor sick of the whole messy affair. So the language of politics, the language of culture and the language of religion spoke in one chorus that Jesus was King to the chagrin of the Jewry.

CONVERSION ON THE CROSS

The four soldiers now divided the spoil — the poor worldly belongings of a man who owned almost nothing except his raiment. The headgear, the cloak-like outer garment, the girdle and the sandals, each one took one because it was more or less of the same value. But for the seamless inner garment, the most valuable of all, they cast lot.

Even as they were casting the dice, they heard a prayer from the cross: "**Father, forgive them, for they do not know what they do.**"

Why should the one who forgave others their sin now ask the Father to forgive sin? Because according to the Trinitarian concept any sin against the Son is a sin against deity and hence against the Father. If only they knew who he really was, their hands would have refrained from the guilt of his blood.

What followed was a mockers' parliament led by the henchmen of the chief priests and the Pharisees. They had not forgotten the power of his whip that drove away those selling their wares inside the temple three years ago and his lashing reply that still rang in their ears, "If you destroy this temple, I will raise it up in three days."

St Matthew records the three 'ifs' of the mockers which remind us of the three 'ifs' of Satan tempting Jesus in the wilderness:

"You who are going to destroy the temple and build it in

three days, save yourself! Come down from the cross, if you are the Son of God!"

"He saved others, but he can't save himself! He's the King of Israel! Let him come down now from the cross, and we will believe in him." (If implied: if you come down, we will believe).

"He trusts in God. Let God rescue him now if he wants him, for he said, `I am the Son of God.'"

The Jewish leaders mock him, the soldiers mock him, and now they were joined by one of the two robbers crucified with him. That robber has only a few more hours to live, but how he squanders his life's opportunity!

In stark contrast, fear of God grips the other, leading to understanding and seeing the truth that God projects before his eyes. Lying on the cross, he had a rare glimpse of the kingdom of God. Overtaken by a strong moral sense which he lacked all these years, he rebukes his accomplice, "Being in the same punishment, don't you fear God? This man has done nothing amiss."

Tradition names the impenitent thief Gestas and the penitent thief Dysmas; there is always hope for the one who has the fear of God, and those without are on the highway to hell.

Now comes one of the most touching scenes in the whole of the Scriptures: Then he said, "Jesus, remember me when you come into your kingdom."

Jesus answered him, "**I tell you the truth, today you will be with me in paradise.**"

Pause and think. Three crosses and three deaths. One of the dying tells another dying, 'Remember me when you come into your kingdom. A ridiculously absurd scene, unless the man in the very deep of his consciousness is convinced Jesus is the Son of God.

Three crosses, three deaths: one dying in sin, one forgiven and dying to sin, and one dying for sin, for the sin of the world.

Three crosses, one death, one eternal life and one life-giving life.

What led to the conversion of the penitent one? Living in Palestine, he must have heard from so many about Jesus Christ; how he healed the blind, how he healed the deaf, how he healed the dumb, how he cleansed the lepers; he must have seen the large crowds that followed Jesus; only a few hours ago, he saw the heart-rending scene of the daughters of Jerusalem wailing over him; and he heard the prophetic warning of the impending calamity that would befall Jerusalem which sounded so true in his heart.

In excruciating pain on the cross, all that Jesus uttered was a prayer of forgiveness and love for his tormentors. The majesty and serenity that hallowed his face deeply impressed him, and he was convinced that this man was no ordinary mortal. His belated realisation and faith in the person of Jesus led him to spiritual illumination. While he looks to a future kingdom, Jesus promises Paradise today through him and with him. If his first utterance on the cross has been one of self-forgetfulness, his second utterance has been the most gracious spiritual lesson on life after death.

Where was St John when this touching scene was enacted on Golgotha? We saw him at the chief priest's house and later at the Pretorium, and then he left the scene unnoticed. He must have gone to bring Jesus' mother and the women of Galilee who accompanied him on his last journey to Jerusalem, for a mournful farewell to Jesus. Alas, the disciples who boasted they would lay down their lives for him were nowhere to be seen.

BEHOLD YOUR MOTHER

Jesus may have been on the cross for over two hours when his mother and the Galilean women accompanied by the beloved disciple arrive at Golgotha. And St. John resumes his eyewitness account: Near the cross of Jesus stood his mother, his mother's sister (Salome), Mary the wife of Clopas and Mary Magdalene. When Jesus saw his mother and the disciple he loved standing nearby he said to his mother, "**Woman, behold your son, and to the disciple,** ``Behold, your mother."

Once more we see on the cross his utter self-forgetfulness and his thoughtfulness for others. Where was the need to entrust Mary to the care of the beloved disciple if Jesus had brothers and sisters? As we have seen it was the Jewish practice to refer to one's cousins as brothers and sisters, and in that sense Jesus had brothers and sisters, but Mary had no other children apart from Jesus. So the honour of looking after Jesus' mother goes to the next of kin, Mary's sister Salome's son and Jesus' own beloved disciple, whom we know as St John.

The chain of relations does not stop there. Clopas also called Alphaeus is the brother of Joseph, the foster father of Jesus and hence his wife, often referred to in the gospels as the other Mary, the aunt of Jesus. Thus we have five cousins of Jesus among the twelve Apostles: two sons of Salome and Zebedee (James and John), and three sons of Alphaeus and Mary (James, Judas surnamed Lebbaeus or Thaddaeus, and Simon surnamed Zelotes or Cananaean).

St John took his commission seriously and almost immediately led Mother Mary away from the scene of unutterable woe to the shelter of his home. Through her soul pierced the sword — the ordeal of a mother to see her son hanging on a cross. Why do the righteous suffer and the wicked prosper? Why does the righteous God allow such sufferings in the life of righteous men and women?

Remember, like the fattened calf kept for slaughter, the wicked are kept for the Day of Judgement. In God's scale of justice, there is recompense for the righteous and hope of eternal life. The cynic may laugh at the idea but he will surely meet his Maker in dismay.

MY GOD, MY GOD ... !

Now there was darkness from the sixth hour to the ninth hour (12-3 pm). Jesus had been on the cross for three hours (9 am to 12 pm) burning in the blazing sun as the burnt offering of God. The time has come for him to offer himself as the sin offering bearing the burden of the sins of humanity. Every sin is an affront to the holiness of the Father and the justice of God demands that no sin goes unpunished. So Jesus takes upon himself the outpouring of God's wrath against sin, thus cut off from the fellowship of the Father for a short while. The human mind can never fathom the agony of the Son of God at that moment, the very thought of which turned his sweat into blood at Gethsemane.

Cut off from the fellowship of Heaven, cut off from the fellowship of man, cut off from the fellowship of every soul, he uttered at the end of his three-hour ordeal:

"My God, my God, why has thou forsaken me?"

While St Matthew uses the Judean or Galilean dialect (Eli, Eli, lama sabakthani) St Mark uses the Syriac form (Eloi, Eloi, ...)

A thousand years ago, King David foresaw the crucifixion and agony of Christ, as revealed by the Holy Spirit, and wrote Psalm 22, which so aptly and prophetically describes the spirit of triumph emerging from the tragedy. A unique first person account, so illumining:

My God, my God, why have you forsaken me

Why are you so far from saving me,
so far from the words of my groaning
But I am a worm and not a man,
scorned by men and despised by the people.
All those who see me mock me;
they hurl insults, shaking their heads:
He trusts in the Lord;
let the Lord rescue him. Let him deliver him,
since he delights in him ...
Many bulls surround me;
strong bulls of Bashan encircle me.
Roaring lions tearing their prey
open their mouths like water,
and all my bones are out of joint.
My heart has turned to wax;
it melted away within me.
My strength is dried up like a potsherd,
and my tongue sticks to the roof of my mouth;
you lay me in the dust of death.
Dogs have surrounded me,
they have pierced my hands and feet.
I can count all my bones;
people stare and gloat over me.
They divide my garments among them
and cast lots for my clothing.
And the ends of the earth
will remember and turn to the Lord

and he rules over the nations.

And all the rich of the earth will feast and worship;
all who go down to the dust will kneel before him —
those who cannot keep themselves alive.

Posterity will serve him;
future generations will be told about the Lord.
They will proclaim his righteousness
to a people yet unborn —
for he has done it.

IT IS FINISHED

The darkness at noon — argues critics Wetstein, Strauss and Keim — is as metaphor! Nothing is more specious than that, since all the synoptic gospel writers record it. An equally specious argument would be that your great-great-grandfather never lived because he had left behind no historical evidence to prove his existence! An equally counter-productive debate is whether an eclipse caused the darkness. The darkness the gospel writers refer to is a supernatural phenomenon which could have a natural cause — eclipse or no eclipse.

At the nick of time enters St John to record the fifth utterance of Jesus on the cross. The friendly Galilean folks who accompanied Jesus on his last journey were standing afar off unable to watch the sight any longer. St John moves closer to the cross and hears the next utterance of Jesus:

"I thirst."

St John alone among the gospel writers records this, explaining the act of the soldier, who rushed to Jesus with a sponge filled with rough wine and put it to his lips with the reed of hyssop, a common Palestinian plant that grows up to three feet. Other soldiers, unable to understand the import of his previous utterance, thought he was calling Elijah. They said let's see whether Elijah would come down from heaven to save him.

Having accomplished all that he came to accomplish, Jesus said:

"It is finished."

Human Redemption is no more a promise but a reality. No longer do men have to fear the terrible consequences of sin or hell, which is eternal separation from God. And his sacrifice is for all humanity and his Redemption for mankind.

With a loud voice, Jesus said: **"Father into thy hands, I commit my spirit."** The next moment, he bowed his head. The last two sayings on the cross came in quick succession.

The manner of His death — the power with which He uttered his last word and the ease and grace with which He gave up His Spirit — made a profound impression on the Roman centurion.

"Truly, he was the Son of God," commented the centurion, praising God.

That same moment, the veil of the temple was torn from top to bottom, the veil that is 60 feet long and 30 feet wide and thick as the palm of the hand, the veil that could employ two hundred Priests in lifting it ceremonially and fixing it.

That same moment, the earth shook and rocks split, and the soldiers were terrified.

No less than four independent testimonies confirm that some great catastrophe, betokening the impending destruction of the temple had occurred in the sanctuary about this time. Tacitus, Josephus, the Talmud, and the earliest Christian tradition confer on this point.

Josephus speaks of the mysterious extinction of the middle and chief light in the Golden Candlestick, forty years before the destruction of the temple; and both he and the Talmud refer to a supernatural opening by themselves of the temple gates that had been previously closed, which was regarded as a portent of the coming destruction of the temple.

His death rent the curtain to the Holy of Holies granting mankind access to the presence of the Living and Holy God. Because of His atoning sacrifice, heaven's gateway is now open to you. The gateway to the Omnipotent, Omniscient and Omnipresent God!

BLOOD AND WATER

In Palestine, the Jewish Sabbath was about to begin. The chief priests and elders were worried that it was unlawful that bodies hang on the cross that day. But whether it was lawful to hand over God's anointed to be crucified did not bother their seared conscience!

So the Jewry asked the governor to break the legs of the crucified to hasten their death. But Pilate could not believe that Jesus was dead so soon; he summoned the centurion on whose word he granted them permission.

The soldiers broke the legs of the two robbers but when they came to Jesus they found him dead already. To make doubly sure, one of them pierced his side with a lance and forthwith came blood and water.

The ringing sincerity with which St John reports this touching moment transports the reader to the scene where he sees before his eyes the Roman soldier in action, swinging the lance into the air and then piercing the rib of Jesus with a thud and the springing fountain of blood and water gushing out.

The scene made a deep impression in the mind of the beloved disciple that he transcreates it with such effect that electrifies the mind of the reader. And with all his earnestness, he attests: "He who has witnessed this is the one who writes this, and his testimony is true."

Three scenes on this longest day of the earth far outweigh all criticism against the Person and Deity of Jesus: the conversion of the thief on the cross reported by Luke, the testimony of the Roman centurion reported by St Matthew and St Mark, and the fountain of blood and water from the body of Jesus Christ reported by St John. Carefully studied and meditated upon, they reveal the character and person of the One who split history into BC and AD.

Christ died broken-hearted as John's narrative shows. When the lance pierced first the lung filled with blood and then the pericardium filled with serous fluid, there flowed from the wound this double stream, which is a rare medical phenomenon.

Another surprise awaited Pilate that day when a member of the Jewish Council boldly asked permission to bury the body of Jesus. By reputation, wealth and scriptural erudition, he ranked among the foremost. This man, Joseph of Arimathea, was a secret disciple seeking the kingdom of God. His boldness must have impressed Pilate, who failed to display his own at the trial of the Nazarene.

In his new rock-hewn tomb, wherein no man was ever laid, he decided to bury the body of Jesus. His friend Nicodemus had gone to buy spices and linen cloths, while the beloved disciple went to bring Mother Mary for the last rites.

When they all reassembled, the cross was lowered and laid on the ground; the cruel nails drawn out and the ropes unloosened; his wounds were carefully washed and his body wrapped in a clean linen cloth; and reverentially his sacred body carried to the tomb, attended by invisible angelic legions.

At the entrance to the tomb within, there was a court, nine feet square, where the bier was deposited and the last rites performed. Nicodemus had brought a roll of myrrh and aloes, in the well-known fragrant mixture for anointing or burying. None of the disciples were there, except St John who alone stood at the foot of the cross.

A motley crowd of four women, the three Marys and Salome, and three men, John, Joseph and Nicodemus, were the sole representatives of humanity at the burial of the Son of Man. It was so at his birth, a flock of shepherds and later three wise men were divinely chosen to herald it. It was so at his dedication in the temple, the godly Simeon and Anna were divinely ordained to witness it. Of course, the host of angels and archangels made their invisible presence felt to those who have invisible eyes to see.

The linen cloth in which the body was wrapped was torn into swathes into which the body, limb by limb, was bound between layers of myrrh and aloes, the head being wrapped in a napkin. And they laid him in the niche of the tomb and went out, rolling a great stone (golel) to close the entrance and a smaller stone (dopheq) for support, which was the practice. It would be where the Jewish authorities affix the seal so that the slightest disturbance might become visible.

As the sunset and the cool breeze blew over the still sepulchere that evening, many in Palestine thought that was the end of the story.

SEEING IS BELIEVING

Mary Magdalene woke up very early in the morning, and walked to the sepulchre along with the Galilean women — the other Mary, Salome and Joanna. Unable to control her grief, she ran ahead of others. When she reached the sepulchre, she found that the huge stone at the entrance had been rolled aside; she peered in and found that the body of Jesus was not there. In panic, she ran to report it to Peter and John.

On the way, the Galilean women wondered who would remove the huge stone at the tomb so that they could anoint the sacred body with the spices they have pains-takingly prepared. One reaching the tomb, they too found the stone removed; and they went in but did not find the body of Jesus. Standing perplexed, they saw two men in shining white garments like lightning, and the women bowed their faces.

"Why do you seek the living among the dead? He is not here, he has risen!" said the men.

The women came back and told the eleven, who did not believe. Curiosity-driven Peter and John ran to the sepulchre, and on the way the youthful John outran Peter. Having won the race, John wanted his elder to win the trophy, and waited. John bent over and looked in at the strips of linen lying there. Meanwhile, Peter arrived and went into the tomb followed by John; they saw the linen and the head cloth folded up by itself and lying exactly where Joseph and Nicodemus had left it on Friday. The linen and the head cloth was untouched by human hand, as if the body of Jesus had escaped through it. John saw and believed, Peter was overawed yet not certain. Both returned to their abode.

Mary stood alone outside the sepulchre, weeping, as she was in no mood to leave the place. She bent over to look into the tomb, and saw two angels in shining garment, where Jesus' body had been, one at the head and the other at the foot.

They tenderly asked her, "Woman, why are you crying?"

"They have taken my Lord away, and I don't know where they have put him."

When she turned, she saw another person standing beside her, but because of her grief, she did not understand who it was.

Even more tenderly asked the man, "Woman, why are you crying? Who is it you are looking for?"

Thinking he was the gardener, she said, "Sir, if you have carried him away, tell me where you have put him, and I will get him."

"Mary."

She could not believe her ears; she turned and cried out, "Rabboni" (Teacher in Aramaic). In that dramatic turnaround, her tears and sorrow vanished like dew drops in the rising sun and joy unspeakable filled her heart as she grasped the reality of Resurrection, which is to see the living God before your eyes, even the God who cares.

She would have grabbed the feet of Jesus in worshipful adoration, but was restrained.

"Do not hold on to me, for I have not yet returned to my Father. Go instead to my brothers and tell them, `I am returning to my Father and your Father, to my God and your God'."

Who was the world's first evangelist — the one who was sent to proclaim Jesus rose from the dead even to the Apostles — and the one who has seen the Risen Lord before others? And whoever said women are unfit to be evangelists?

So broken-hearted was Mary that the Good Lord did not have the heart to leave her grieving and ascend to the Father. He first heals the broken-hearted and in the process blesses her with the first Post-Resurrection appearance.

"I have seen the Lord!" Mary declares confidently to the Apostles. Is that amazing to you that s(h)e who seeks God truly finds him?

That same spring day early afternoon, two disciples left Jerusalem by the Western gate; a 25- minute walk took them to the plateau, leaving the bloodstained city behind. The air grew fresher and fresher with every step upward, the scent of the mountain and the breeze from the far-off sea mingling. A thirty-minute climb brought Bethlehem in view; and a quarter of an hour ahead of the rocky hill was a lovely valley. The path gently climbed to a height on which stood Emmaus. Equidistant from Emmaus lay two towns, Lifta on the right and Kolonieh on the left; and roads from these two meet in semi-circles a quarter of a mile south of Emmaus (Hammoza). Emmaus, an oasis of orange and lemon gardens, olive groves and luscious fruit trees amidst the hilly region. Emmaus, an ideal setting for scriptural exposition.

Where the two roads met a stranger accosted the disciples.

"What are you discussing while walking?" The stranger asked, perhaps to get noticed.

They stood face downcast in sorrow. Cleopas and his companion, left unnamed, asked him, "Are you a visitor to Jerusalem, the only one who does not know what the whole city is talking about?"

"What things?"

"About Jesus of Nazareth. He was a prophet, powerful in word and deed before God and all the people. The chief priests and our rulers handed him over to be sentenced to death, and they crucified him; but we had hoped that he was the one who was going to redeem Israel. And what is more, it is the third day since all this took place. Some of our women amazed us. They went to the tomb, but did not find his body. They came and told us that they had seen a vision of angels, who said he was alive. Then some of our companions went to the tomb and found it just as the women had said, but him they did not see."

This reply gives us a three-fold understanding of the times in which they lived. It was an oppressive society, politically and economically. Their own religious leaders and the rich oppressed them; Imperial Rome took away the best of grains and farm produce that people felt doubly oppressed. A great Messianic hope was building around the person of Jesus. What the people witnessed on that fateful Friday was not the death of a Prophet, but the death of their Messianic hope — and a common grief they all shared.

The second aspect is the importance of the third day in the mindset of the Jew. Abraham reached Mount Moria on the third day to sacrifice his son; Jonah was in the belly of the fish for three days; God never leaves the just more than three days in anguish; the spirit of the dead was believed to hover around the body for three days.

The third aspect is the gaining credibility of the Galilean women's report as more and more people discover the truth of the empty tomb and the linen wrappings lying untouched.

"How foolish you are, and how slow of heart to believe all that the prophets have spoken! Did not the Christ have to suffer these things and then enter his glory?" And beginning with Moses and all the Prophets, he explained to them what was said in all the Scriptures concerning Christ.

As the three reached Emmaus, the stranger was about to go further, but the two persuaded him to stay for the night. They laid the table for the stranger who expounded the scriptures; he took bread, gave thanks, broke it and gave it to them. Then their eyes were opened, and they recognised Christ. And he disappeared from their sight.

What a God who talks with them and walks with them and communes with them!

"Were not our hearts burning within us while he talked with us on the road and opened the scriptures to us?" they asked each other; and they rushed back to Jerusalem unable to contain the joy of meeting the Lord.

When the two reached Jerusalem, they found the Apostles assembled and Peter was sharing how the Lord appeared to him. As soon as he had finished, the two had a life-transforming experience to share.

While the two were still talking about him, how he broke the bread, gave it to them, how their eyes were opened, and how he disappeared from their sight, Jesus himself stood amidst them and greeted:

"Peace be with you."

They were startled by the suddenness of his appearance. They thought it was a ghost.

"Why are you troubled, and why do you doubt? Look at my hands and my feet. It is I myself. Touch me and see; a ghost does not have flesh and bones, as you see I have."

He showed them the nail prints on his hands and feet; but in the transport of their joy, they could not believe. The rational mind needs time to adjust to the new reality.

"Do you have anything to eat?"

They gave him a broiled fish, and he took it and ate it in their presence.

"This is what I told you while I was still with you: Everything must be fulfilled that is written about me in the Law of Moses, the Prophets and the Psalms."

Then he opened their minds so that they could understand the Scriptures.

He told them, "This is what is written: The Christ will suffer and rise from the dead on the third day, and repentance and forgiveness of sins will be preached in his name to all nations, beginning at Jerusalem. You are witnesses of these things. I am going to send you what my Father promised (The Holy Spirit); but stay in the city until you have been clothed with power from on high."

It was an eventful Easter day. But Thomas, one of the Apostles, was conspicuous by his absence when the Lord appeared.

"We have seen the Lord," declared the disciples to Thomas, who countered:

"Unless I see the nail marks in his hands and put my finger where the nails were, and put my hands into his side, I will not believe."

The next Sunday, they assembled in the same house, behind locked doors, and Jesus appeared amidst them greeting, "Peace be unto you!"

Then he said to Thomas, "Put your finger here; see my hands. Reach out your hand and put it into side. Stop doubting and believe."

"My Lord and my God," exclaimed Thomas as he stood bewildered.

"Because you have seen me, you have believed; blessed are those who have not seen and yet have believed."

Thomas confessed Jesus as his Lord and God. Lord is someone who has authority over you; unless He is your Lord, he cannot be your God.

The sceptic-turned believer, St. Thomas' confession ranks among the greatest confessions, like that of Peter at Caesaria Philippi ("You are the Christ"), or that of the penitent robber

("Jesus remember me in your kingdom") or that of the Roman centurion at the foot of the cross ("Truly, he was the Son of God").

Old temptations diehard! Fisherman Peter told his comrades at the Sea of Galilee — Sons of Zebedee James and John, Thomas Didymus, Nathaniel Bartholomew of Cana, and two other disciples — "I am going out to fish."

The temptation to go back to their old trade was too strong. "We are with you," responded the others.

There is something in Simon that elicited quick response from his listeners, maybe his powerful voice, maybe his deep conviction, maybe his force of character, maybe his physical frame. But whatever, he is born to lead — at times to mislead.

The Apostles of high calling were backsliding into their old ways! No wonder they caught nothing all night despite their proficiency in the craft.

They had a visitor early next morning, asking, "Friends, haven't you any fish?"

'No', they admitted their desperation.

"Throw your net on the right side," said the visitor, as if he saw a school of fish moving around.

When they did, they could not draw the net because of the number of fish they caught.

Three years ago, on the same shore, perhaps in the same place, Jesus called them to be fishers of men; and they left everything and followed Jesus. On the same shore, now they leave Jesus behind and go back into the same trade.

"It is the Lord," John told Peter, because he remembered it is the replay of the same story.

Peter cannot delay. Wrapping his outer garment around him, he slips into the water to meet the Lord before anyone did.

John is ever the first to understand; Peter is ever the first to act; and they form such a perfect pair.

The other disciples followed in the boat, which is about a hundred yards away.

When they reached the shore, they saw a fire of burning coals with fish on it, and some bread.

"Bring some of the fish you have just caught," said Jesus.

Simon dragged the net ashore and counted 153 large fish (the same number as the total species of fish); and yet the net did not break.

"Come and have breakfast," he invited them. He took the bread and gave it to them, and also the fish. A God who serves!

Jesus had some business with Simon. After they finished eating, he called him and said, "Simon son of John, do you truly love me more than these?" (which means more than everything else in the world).

"Yes, Lord, you know that I love you."

"Feed my lambs."

Again Jesus said, "Simon son of John, do you truly love me?"

"Yes, Lord, you know that I love you."

"Take care of my sheep."

The third time he said, "Simon son of John, do you love me?"

The English translation is inadequate to portray the dilemma which Peter faces. In Greek, there are four words to express love: **agape**, which is infinite love that God alone is capable of; **storgey**, which is love without seeking rewards like a mother's love; **philo**, which is a friend's love; and **eros**, which is physical love.

Jesus used agape the first two times in the sense 'Be perfect as my Father is perfect' and philo the third time as if lowering his expectation.

Asking the third time almost the same question saddened

Simon, because the memory of his three-fold denial weighed heavy in his mind.

"Lord, you know all things; you know that I love you," Simon said not boastfully this time but trustingly — trusting the Lord who knows all things.

"Feed my sheep."

Peter is re-commissioned to the job he was designated, but not without eliciting a confession each for his denials. What a God who restores the failing!

"I tell you the truth, when you were younger you dressed yourself and went where you wanted; but when you are old you will stretch out your hands, and someone else will dress you and lead you where you do not want to go."

Jesus is revealing that Simon Peter will stretch out his hand and will be crucified as Jesus was, to the glory of the kingdom.

Simon was curious to know how John would fare.

"If I want him to remain alive until I return, what is that to you?"

Do not expect the sovereign God to play the soothsayer. In his infinite wisdom, He conceals what ought to remain concealed, and reveals what ought to be revealed.

Jesus did many other things, writes St. John, which if he wrote the world could not contain.

Jesus appeared to the Apostles during 40 days, imparting them insights into the kingdom of God. "It is not for you to know the times or dates the Father has set by his own authority. But you will receive power when the Holy Spirit comes upon you..." The disciples have to live in the power of the Holy Spirit, who is their guide and teacher.

On the 40th day since Resurrection, he walked with them from Mount Olives to Bethany, and he lifted up his hands and blessed them, and he was taken up before their very eyes, and a cloud hid him from their sight.

They were looking intently up into the sky as he was going, when suddenly two men dressed in white stood beside them.

"Men of Galilee, why do you stand here looking into the sky? The same Jesus, who has been taken from you into heaven, will come back in the same way you have seen him go into heaven."

THE UNIQUE PRESENCE

This section is meant for people who love contemplation. What is unique about the person of Jesus Christ? "Man never spoke like him," said the temple guards sent to arrest him. His rhetoric elegance and the beauty of exposition mesmerised the audience. The sparkle in his eyes, the glow on his face, the unkempt flowing hair forming an arc around his temple, his chiseled rainbow cheeks that defy carnal experience and his reverberating beard that drew instant attention of children, fastened their eyes on him.

The world has seen philosophers, emperors, statesmen, scientists, humanists; but no one ever claimed what Jesus did: "I and my Father (God) are one." At the heart of his message are the unique 7 'I ams': `I am the Light of the World, `I am the Living Water, `I am the Bread of Life', `I am the Life and Resurrection', `I am the Good Shepherd', `I am the Way, the Truth and the Life', and `I am the Vine and you are the branches'.

These 7 'I ams' are the key to understanding who Jesus Christ is.: In him dwelt God's light and in his person he revealed God. He imparts the Spirit of God metaphorically called the living water; his word nourishes the inner life as bread nourishes the physical life. Invisibly he is present with every believer guiding him like a good shepherd. He is the way to the Father, the way to truth and the way to eternal life. And he gifts new life (spiritual life) to every believer as branches growing in the vine.

A synoptic biography of Jesus Christ could have been written some 600 years before he was born. The Old Testament carries nearly

250 Messianic prophecies that he would be born in a manger in Bethlehem, that a bright star would herald his birth, that wise men from the East would visit him, that he would preach in Galilee, that he would teach in parables, that he would enter Jerusalem triumphantly on the colt of an ass, that he would be cut off at the prime of his youth, that he would be crucified amidst criminals, that his garments would be divided among the soldiers (who crucified him), that he will be buried in a wealthy man's grave and that he would rise again on the third day. There never lived another man of whom it could be so said. His birth, his life, his ministry, his teaching, his passion, his death, his burial and his resurrection are unique.

Jesus Christ is unique because he can take you to the presence of the living and eternal God. "I stand at the door and knock. If anyone hears my voice and opens the door, I will come in and sup with him, and he with me... If anyone loves me, he will obey by teaching (commandment). My Father will love him, and we will come to him and make our home with him... Come unto me who are weary and burdened, and I will give you rest... Behold, I am with you till the end of the world." (Read: Rev 3:20, St John 14:23, Matthew 11:28, and Matthew 28:20).

Words that no man ever uttered, no teacher ever taught, no philosopher ever expounded, words that could be tried and tested. This invisible but unique presence of the living God in human heart is the uniqueness of the teaching and person of Christ.

THE ROADMAP TO THE KINGDOM

The rhetoric and imagery of Jesus drew large crowds. "Consider the lilies of the field, how they grow: they neither toil nor spin; and yet I say to you that even Solomon in all his glory was not arrayed like one of these. Now if God so clothes the grass of the field, which today is, and tomorrow is thrown into the oven, will he not much more clothe you, O you of little faith. Therefore do not worry, saying, `what shall we eat' or `what shall we drink' or `what shall we wear' `For after all these things the gentiles seek. For your heavenly Father knows that you need all these things. But seek first the kingdom of God and His righteousness, and all these things shall be added to you."

That was Jesus telling his audience that the first duty of every citizen of the Kingdom of God is to seek God who will meet all his needs because He is a loving Father.

"And when you pray, you shall not be like the hypocrites. For they love to pray standing in the synagogues and on the corners of the streets, that they may be seen by men. Assuredly, I say to you, they have their reward. But you, when you pray, go into your room and when you have shut your door, pray to your Father who is in the secret place; and your Father who sees in secret will reward you openly. And when you pray, do not use vain repetitions as the heathen do. For they think that they will be heard for their many words. Therefore do not be like them. For your Father knows the things you have need of before you ask him."

Prayer is establishing a loving relationship with the Father which is nothing short of empowerment. But the histrionics of the hypocrites is the antithesis of prayer.

"Do not lay up for yourselves treasures on earth, where moth and rust destroy and where thieves break in and steal; but lay up for yourselves treasures in heaven, where neither moth nor rust destroys and where thieves do not break in and steal. For where your treasure is, there your heart will be also."

Learn to treasure the Word and you will indeed find the meaning of life. What folly that some men trust in treasures that play vanishing tricks in a transient world.

"You are the light of the world. A city that is set on a hill cannot be hidden. Nor do they light a lamp and put it under a basket but on a lamp stand, and it gives light to all who are in the house. Let your light so shine before men, that they may see your good works and glorify your Father in heaven."

The children of the Kingdom practise doing good for the glory of their Father which is the chief goal of their life. One candle light can kindle a thousand candles and one godly person can transform first his home and family, then his neighbourhood and his town and finally the society at large.

"A certain man went down from Jerusalem to Jericho, and fell among thieves, who stripped him of his clothing, wounded him, and departed, loving him half dead. Now by chance a certain priest came down that road. And when he saw him, he passed by on the other side. Likewise a Levite, when he arrived at the place, came and looked, and passed by on the other side. But a certain Samaritan, as he journeyed, came where he was. And when he saw him, he had compassion. So he went to him and bandaged his wounds, pouring on oil and wine; and he set him on his own animal, brought him to an inn, and took care of him. On the next day, when he departed, he took out two denarii, gave them to the inn-keeper, and said to him, 'Take care of him; and whatever more you spend, when I come again, I will repay you.' So which of these three do you think was neighbour to him who fell among the thieves? Three types of theologies are at work in the story - Mafia, Sophia and Gloria. The school of Mafia, where the robber belongs, believes in brute force. The school of Sophia, where the Priest and the Levite belong, believes in the rational way. And the school of Gloria, where the Samaritan belongs, believes in compassion.

The irony of the story is that the priest who ought to lead men to holiness leave the wounded to his predicament because he was afraid the man might die any moment defiling him. The juxtaposition of the humanity of the Samaritan and the inhumanity of religion is the hallmark of Jesus' oratorical excellence.

"What did you go out in the wilderness to see? A reed shaken by the wind? But what did you go out to see? A man clothed in soft garments? Indeed, those who wear soft clothing are in King's houses. But what did you go out to see? A prophet? Yes, I say to you, and more than a prophet."

A lively profile of John the Baptist, designed to raise curiosity and suspense as part of a communication strategy to confront audience lethargy.

"Foxes have holes, and birds of the air have nests, but the Son of Man has nowhere to lay His head," a statement of the revolutionary Grachhi brothers of Rome made famous by Jesus who identifies himself with the under-privileged of the earth.

"You follow me, and let the dead bury their own dead", Jesus spoke to a disciple lacking the single-mindedness for the Kingdom.

That was the road map to the Kingdom in a 7-fold step: seek, pray, treasure, shine, honour and forsake.

www.ingramcontent.com/pod-product-compliance
Lightning Source LLC
Chambersburg PA
CBHW030231170426
43201CB00006B/185